HURRY HOME

HURRY HOME

novella and short stories
by
Ann Scott Knight

FOUR WAY BOOKS
Marshfield

Copyright © 1999 Ann Scott Knight
No part of this book may be used or reproduced in any manner
without written permission except in the case of brief quotations
embodied in critical articles and reviews. Please direct all inquiries to:

Four Way Books
PO Box 607
Marshfield, MA 02050

Library of Congress Catalogue Card Number: 98-72337
ISBN 1-884800-24-6
Cover art: painting by Pedro Bonnin:
Neither Night Nor Day, oil, 1994
Cover and text design: The Creative Team

Four Way Books is a division of Friends of Writers, Inc.,
a Vermont-based not-for-profit organization. Publication of this book
was made possible by generous support from individual donors.

Acknowledgments

This is a work of fiction. Names, characters, places and incidents either
are the products of the author's imagination or are used fictitiously,
and any resemblance to actual persons, living or dead, events,
or locales is entirely coincidental.

Several of these stories have appeared,
in slightly different form, in the following magazines:
The Chattahoochee Review, "Night Games";
Four Way Reader #1, "As They Were Then";
The Marlboro Review, "Impossible with Nancy";
Phoebe, "Thin Air";
The South Carolina Review, "The Hand Is Quicker Than the Heart"

I would like to thank the following people for reading these
stories and making insightful and intelligent suggestions:
Howell Draper, Helen Fremont, Dale Neal, Bethany Pray,
Claudia Rankine, Mike Rothburd, and Joan Silber.
I am also grateful to Lewis Buzbee, Lisa Goldfarb,
Ellen Hochschwender, Peter Knight, Futoshi Miyai,
Leslie Reiner, Martha Rhodes, Mary Elsie Robertson, and Virginia Weir.
Thanks also to the Hillsborough County Arts Council for its support.

A Nicola Tatiana King Selection

For Doug
and Thomas

CONTENTS

As They Were Then / 3

Impossible with Nancy / 11

Paradise / 23

Thin Air / 37

The Man with Pointed Ears / 51

Night Games / 63

A Business Trip / 73

The Burglary / 95

Devotion / 107

The Hand Is Quicker Than the Heart / 119

Hurry Home / 139

AS THEY WERE THEN

When I saw the proof sheet, I was surprised that none of the photographs showed my face.

I had let Margie take pictures of me without clothes. She kept her eye to the lens and spoke in a quiet voice, making suggestions. Why not lean back against the pillows? Or wear fish net stockings and a hat with feathers? We had locked the bedroom door to keep her mother out, though she had been busy all afternoon cooking brisket.

✧ ✧ ✧

My father gave me a sports car for my seventeenth birthday. When it arrived from the factory, he wrote the dealer a check for seven thousand dollars. The car was metallic blue, capable of speed, and mine.

I learned to drive with no one's help, by popping the clutch and stalling. My dog Sasha lay behind the seats under the slanting glass hatch back. When I was a hundred miles from home, she threw up onto the carpet. I pulled into an all-night Mobil station near Orlando and used paper towels soaked in windshield cleaner to take away the smell.

The gas station attendant, handsome, just out of high school, talked me into giving him a blow job behind his desk.

✧ ✧ ✧

I chose as the topic of my class presentation *The Feminine Mystique* by Betty Friedan. It was the only feminist book I had heard of. My history teacher encouraged me and helped me with the outline.

On the day of my presentation, I wore a skirt and a new blouse with a lace collar. I stood in front of the class and talked about penis envy, waiting for someone to snicker.

At the end I asked for questions. No one raised their hand. I returned to my seat in the front row and sat with my back to the class. More than anything, I hated the frilly blouse.

✛ ✛ ✛

At the horse show in Brooksville I won the Junior Hunt Seat Equitation class. That night when my roommate fell asleep, I crept out of our room at the Holiday Inn, sneaked down the hall and knocked on Peter Sullivan's door.

He wasn't expecting me but his room was tidy, all his clothes put away in drawers or hung in the closet beside the bathroom. One bedspread was wrinkled from where he'd been lying. On the other bed was an economics text, a spiral notebook and a tan leather briefcase.

He sat on his bed and lay the briefcase like a tray across his knees. Click, click. He opened it and from one of its pockets drew out a condom.

Fifteen minutes later he clapped his hands and said, "Get dressed." As I walked out the door, he was sitting at his desk with his textbook open, underlining an important passage with a yellow marker.

✛ ✛ ✛

At eight o'clock on Christmas Eve, my father still wasn't home. My sister sat on the sofa in her green velvet dress. I put on a record, our old holiday favorite—"A Child's Christmas in Wales"—while my brothers fought over one of my father's broken stethoscopes.

Finally, to placate them, my mother said they could open a present. The best presents were saved for morning. She chose the ones they would appreciate least. They ripped off the wrapping only to discover identical sailor suits.

AS THEY WERE THEN

In the middle of dinner my father called from the hospital. He was stuck in the delivery room with a woman giving birth to twins.

I asked to be excused from the table. Judy Pepello, the girl next door, was waiting for me on the golf course. She had stolen Quaaluds from her mother's medicine cabinet. I had stolen Valium.

By the time I woke up the next morning, my father was back at the hospital, delivering another baby. My brothers and sister had emptied their stockings and stuffed themselves sick with candy.

✢ ✢ ✢

Otto, my horse, was a dappled gray thoroughbred. The first time I walked into his stall he bit me on the arm, leaving a yellow apple-shaped bruise. But when he jumped, he was a beauty—ears forward, neck rounded, back arched, knees tucked.

One afternoon I galloped him across the pastures behind the barn, herding imaginary cows. Afterwards, I washed him with the hose and walked him for fifteen minutes. He was still sweating when I left him in his stall. The barn hands came through the aisles, feeding the horses a special bran mash. Otto ate too quickly and then drank water. In the night he got colic and twisted a gut. When his screams finally woke up the stable manager, who lived across the paddock, it was too late to save him.

Though my father had taken out an insurance policy in case of accidental death, by then I was seventeen, preparing for college, too old for another horse.

✢ ✢ ✢

Amy Randall, my best friend, was the number one tennis player under seventeen in the state. After I quit riding, I spent afternoons watching her practice with the pro. I sat on the hood of her car, parked under an oak tree beside the country club courts. I rolled down all the windows and listened, at top decibel, to the cassettes her brother had made her.

Afterwards we went to the country club restaurant and ordered cokes and french fries and charged them to our fathers. I always broke the dress code—by wearing flip flops or a see-through shirt. No one dared to kick me out. My grandfather was the richest man in town.

✢ ✢ ✢

During spring break, I told my parents I was staying in a hotel on Indian Rocks Beach with friends. Instead I spent the first four days of April with Jack Jenkins in his condominium.

The first day we ate fruit, the second day drank fruit juice, the third day we ate nothing and drank only water. I wrote journal entries for him to read: erotic daydreams which prompted us to sex. He refused to turn on the air conditioner and we sweated toxins out of our pores.

On the fourth morning we broke fast with a mound of steamed broccoli. By then my appetite was lost.

✢ ✢ ✢

"I won first prize in Latin," I said to my mother.

She stood in the kitchen, stirring sugar into her coffee.

"I'm going to shave my head bald," I said.

She smiled, sipped the coffee and held the china cup with her little finger outstretched.

"I'm pregnant and the father is a black man."

She looked at me. I was ready to smile, even laugh. She set the cup back down in its saucer, re-cinched her quilted robe and as she brought the coffee into the breakfast room, she reached over and lightly tickled my neck.

☩ ☩ ☩

My sister left her teeth marks, like fingerprints, wherever she went. She bit the usual things—her nails, the ends of pencils. She also, at the age of twelve, bit children who played with her too roughly.

Imagine my surprise when the new young priest, who taught sixth grade divinity, came to our house for dinner. When I shook his hand, I recognized the bite mark, a perfect circle of tiny scabs, on the flesh just above his wrist.

☩ ☩ ☩

Amy wasn't a masculine girl but something kept her from being successful with boys. The summer before we went to college—she to Madison, I to Santa Cruz—we spent every day together and she fell in love with me. One night at the beach she kissed my mouth. It was exactly like being kissed by a boy.

For hours she lay beside me, touching my breasts. Only once did I attempt to touch hers. My hand recoiled from the rubbery feel.

My body reacted to her touch the way it reacted to any touch, with deep longing and numbness.

☩ ☩ ☩

My mother dropped a china cup on the floor. After trying in vain to glue it back together, she put the pieces in a large straw basket where she kept her remnants. The basket was like a cobra's nest. Whenever I stuck my hand in, something bit me.

Sometimes my mother took the basket down and fondly looked through its contents: the stem of a champagne flute, a broken cuff link, fragments of decorated Easter eggs and Christmas tree ornaments.

Everyone in the family had contributed to the basket, some more than once. When I was six I had run through the house and knocked over a crystal bird. Every time my mother showed me the pieces, I apologized.

✧ ✧ ✧

The historical society chose my great grandfather's first house, known in our family as the Honeymoon Cottage, for its new headquarters. After the renovation had been completed, an inauguration ceremony was held. My father and my aunt, the two direct descendants, were asked to cut the ribbon and give short speeches.

Amy and I drove by the cottage as the ceremony took place. Under a canopy a few dozen people stood holding programs. In my hand was an egg I'd sworn I was going to throw.

As we got closer, I noticed my brothers, dressed in identical seersucker suits. The way they stood, quiet and unhappy, kept me from throwing the egg. Even when they grew up, I knew they would be as they were then—two obedient unhappy boys, standing on ceremony.

✧ ✧ ✧

My sister refused to go out in the sun. She believed what her ballet teacher told her—that ballerinas needed transparent skin, through which you could see their veins.

When she had to go somewhere on a hot summer day, she ran from the front door to the car. At the beach, she stayed inside doing jigsaw puzzles.

AS THEY WERE THEN

When a black girl enrolled in the ballet school, my sister, all of a sudden, wanted a bikini. She would lie on a chaise lounge in the back yard, reading magazines and working on her tan.

✛ ✛ ✛

General Johnson, a four-star general who lived down the street, told my mother at a cocktail party that if the Communists invaded, they would dig a trench on the golf course, line up all the rich people from the neighborhood and shoot them.

When my mother told me this, I thought for the first time that I wouldn't mind being a Communist.

✛ ✛ ✛

For graduation my grandmother gave me an emerald ring. The stone was a green rarely found in nature, not the green of grass or leaves or the pupils of cats caught in headlights. The ring was so beautiful it caused a commotion. But I could tell it wasn't going to advance my ambitions: make men love me or make me great.

✛ ✛ ✛

Two months after I left for college, on my eighteenth birthday, my father sent a letter.

"I'm sorry to give you this news on your birthday," the letter began. "I'm no longer living at home. Your mother and I are getting a divorce. You know I will always love you."

After a few hours, I called my mother. I imagined her sitting at the table with her basket of broken things, her fingertips lingering over the most jagged bits. She didn't ask me to come home and I didn't offer.

From my window in the dorm I could see the Pacific Ocean. I thought about throwing myself off a cliff. It was a fleeting thought.

IMPOSSIBLE WITH NANCY

It's shimmery hot but I'm afraid to swim Rooster. Sweat drips off my chin and the horse's coat is matted beneath me. Nancy and her horse, Sierra, are already deep in the middle of the swimming hole, and I can't see Sierra anymore, except for his face and a bit of yellowish-gray tail. I'm certain he and Nancy are both about to drown.

"Come in!" Nancy turns and shouts, but we are not supposed to be here, with these horses, far from the barn.

Nancy ducks underwater, hugging her horse's neck, and I hold my breath, frightened, till she comes up again. I've never swum a horse before. All I can think of is losing hold of the mane, getting sucked down into that boiling water and kicked, knocked out cold, by four thrashing hooves.

On the other side of the swimming hole, Sierra's feet touch ground. Nancy is flat, stomach down, stretched the length of his back. She pushes up, laughing, looks down at her shirt. She couldn't care less that it's plastered against her chest.

"Come on, Lucy," she calls. "Miss Priss."

I cluck and squeeze and pull on the rope attached to Rooster's halter. He side steps and blows air out of his nostrils, as if there's something in the water he has to avoid. I reach back and slap him. For a moment he is still and then suddenly he jumps forward, throwing me off balance. I grab mane like I do when approaching a fence and pull my legs up, feel all his legs moving, all four at once. Suddenly we are in the middle, where the water is black and Rooster sinks to his neck. Before I know it, it's over.

His feet touch ground and quickly I have to position myself to come down on his back as he pulls up out of the water.

"Nancy, we're going to get in trouble," I say.

Nancy walks a circle around me and sings, "Every party needs a pooper, that's why we invited you. Party pooper! Party pooper!"

Sometimes I wonder why I've always stood by Nancy, no matter what she does—when she got caught cheating on a geography test, beaten (bloody nose, swollen lip) by her father. When I spend the night at her house, I carefully avoid Dr. Meyer. He's waxed bald with a beard, and most evenings he sits at the edge of his lake, sipping a drink, watching his black swans glide across the water, waiting for (no, it's me, breathlessly anticipating) an alligator to reach up and bite them in half.

"Listen," Nancy says. In the distance hounds are baying. The hunt is closer than we thought. Sierra and Rooster go light on their feet. They are old school horses but they have been on hunts before.

We are out in the open, in the middle of a field. The hunt sounds like it's coming from the trees. I look into the woods and see flashes of red. It's the men—at the head, Mr. Fielding, the master of the hunt, then Mike, our trainer, who specifically told us not to take the horses away from the barn.

We turn and gallop so fast to the barn that I'm weak and laughing, my legs and arms limp. The grooms are all standing around, leaning against the tack room door or sitting on a wooden bench, drinking Cokes and waiting for the hunt to be over. They will have their hands full then. They all stare at Nancy, whose shirt is still wet. She hops off and leads Sierra through the barn to the wash room.

IMPOSSIBLE WITH NANCY

"Shit," she says, discovering a wet pack of Larks in the front pocket of her cut-offs.

"Mike will give us some, or those guys." I point to the grooms. Already one of them is walking over.

Nancy hooks Sierra into the washroom. She turns on the water and picks up the hose. I don't think she's seen the groom, who's now leaning against the wall across from us, but suddenly she straightens up and says, "Do you have a cigarette?"

"Aren't you too young to smoke?" He laughs.

"Humph," she says and turns, holding the hose over Sierra's head. The water runs down his face in a stream. I can't let Rooster stand still so I walk him around in circles in the aisle, waiting for Nancy to soap and rinse her horse.

"How old are you?" the groom asks. He's a greaser—white t-shirt, tan cowboy boots, blonde slicked-back hair. He has that greaser slouch.

"Old enough to know better," says Nancy.

"Is that so?" The groom comes closer.

Nancy turns off the hose and picks up the scraper, ignoring the groom. She scrapes all the excess water off Sierra's back.

Finally I can't wait any longer. "Okay, Nancy. I need to wash Rooster."

The groom walks right into the washroom with Nancy, unhooks the chains from Sierra's halter. "That's right, Nancy. This horse is clean." He puts his hand on Sierra's chest, between his front legs. "But he's warm. He needs to be walked."

"Leave me alone," she says. She walks Sierra down the side aisle of the barn and out into the sun. The groom follows her, laughing, shaking his head. I wash Rooster with a big wet sponge drizzled with Ivory soap. I wash him with the care I usually don't have time for, because the bus that brings us here on weekdays for our lessons is always waiting to take us home.

Behind the barn a blue-and-white striped tent has been pitched for the buffet breakfast after the hunt. The sound of the hounds is closer. Nancy, holding the end of Sierra's lead rope, is standing in front of the bar, talking to the bartender. She comes away with a glass of orange juice that looks half full of vodka.

The groom watches from the door of the barn, his arms crossed over his chest. I admire Nancy's good judgment—she continues to ignore him—and yet, something tells me that if such a boy were watching me, even a greasy stable hand, I would be watching him back.

By now Rooster is cool and dry. I let him eat some grass. He moves his lips, looking for clover. When he finds some, he jerks his head sideways, uproots the clover with a delicate tearing sound. I run my hand down his shoulder. Maybe over the months he's gotten attached to me. He hears me coming when I run off the bus to his stall with a carrot or an apple, which he eats, core, stem and seeds. Once I asked Mike if Rooster were for sale but he just frowned.

"Say."

Rooster has wandered too close to the groom.

"What's wrong with your friend?"

I stare at the groom and blink. Rooster discovers a big patch of clover and yanks me closer. I hear the rip, rip of the roots as he pulls. I am close enough to see the dark horse hairs stuck to the groom's white t-shirt, the dark hairs stuck to the sweat on his neck.

IMPOSSIBLE WITH NANCY

"How old is she?"

"Thirteen," I answer.

He closes his eyes and whistles.

A horn blows. I turn and see the hounds, just beyond the fence, being herded into their pen. The master of the hunt is leading his horse into the barn. The groom straightens, hurries over to a lady in a black silk top hat, holds the braided leather reins while she dismounts. She stands close to him and gives him instructions. Her horse has foam between his lips and all over his chest. He is breathing heavily, blowing through his nostrils, and won't stand still.

Mike goes straight to Nancy. He frowns and points to the barn. Nancy sips her orange juice, gives him a grin, takes her time leading Sierra away. I do the same with Rooster, only much more quickly, before Mike can get to me. The barn is chaotic, grooms yelling, horses too close together, squealing and kicking. I lead Rooster around the back way and go into his stall and peek out the back window. The riders are lined up in front of the bar. Mike has his arm around a man whose right thigh is streaked with red clay. But Mike has his eye on Nancy, who is moving through the paddock on her way to Sierra's stall. Mike brought us to the barn on a Sunday, for the hunt, on the condition that we stay out of sight, a rule Nancy has flagrantly broken.

Melanie Stark, a beautiful girl who owns her own horse and trains with Mike, brings Mike a screwdriver and stands talking to him, fiddling with the end of her long dark braid. She has taken off her jacket and her back is wet, the strap of her bra visible down to the little metal clips. Mike's hand goes to her waist. He looks around to see who is watching (he doesn't see me) then slides his hand down slowly over the tight curve of her breeches, ending with a little pinch, which makes her jump. Mike does this to many girls, often.

Nancy comes into Rooster's stall and stands at the window beside me, peeking out. "Oh." She is fuming. "Let's go to the creek. I can't watch this."

She has two Cokes and an unopened pack of Larks. We race out of the barn, through the paddock, hop the fence and scare the grazing horses, who gallop away. On the way through the ring we trot the *cavaletti*, then canter up and over the two-foot brush. Nancy drops a Coke. "That's yours," she says. I stop and pick it up.

At the creek we smoke ourselves sick and lie on the bank. The palmettos rustle, probably armadillos looking for bugs. Rats with armor, Nancy calls them. Our Cokes are in the water, wedged against stones. Nancy has made sure to separate hers from mine.

She sits up, sings, "Oh, if I had the wings of a buzzard."

"Buzzard," I chime, on cue.

"Off to the woods I would fly."

"Would fly."

"Thar to remain as a buzzard."

"Buzzard."

"Until the day that I die."

"I die, I die," together we finish.

This is a song we sing on the bus. We go through our repertoire, ending with "Bingo," a song that involves a lot of rapid clapping at the end. Occasionally we'll try and sing nicely, but never on the bus, only out here or by the Meyer's lake, where we can let our voices range and try harmonies that sometimes fail and make us laugh.

I end up not drinking my Coke, leaving it in the creek for another day. Maybe by then it won't explode. Instead, I drink the water, squatting down barefooted in the middle of the creek, cupping my hands and holding the water till the flashy bits of dirt settle down and what I drink is mostly clear. Nancy has taken her shirt off to suntan. This is something she's begun doing lately. I don't know where she got the idea, maybe from Louise or Bess, her sisters.

Later in the afternoon, after everybody's left, Mike gives us a ride home. We all three sit in the front seat of his Ford Courier, Nancy in the middle. She sings a few bars of "Norwegian Wood," but I won't sing in front of Mike. He puts his hand on Nancy's bare leg, rubs the inside of her knee, then squeezes, making her scream and jump, pushing me against the door.

"Where did you girls run off to this afternoon?" he asks. He has a Northern accent, talks through his nose.

"We have a secret place," Nancy says.

"Where?" He looks at her, a cigarette between his teeth. She raises her knees and shrugs herself into a ball. He looks at me and I shrug too.

"Where do you girls go?" he teases.

Nancy reaches into his breast pocket, pulls out his Larks and lights two with the car lighter, handing one to me. She has half a pack of her own but I guess she wants to save them.

We're driving through Temple Terrace. "Stop," Nancy says. "Let's get Slurpees."

Mike sighs, turns left and bounces into the Li'l General parking lot, stopping abruptly beside a black pick-up truck with two guns hanging in the rear window rack. "Make it snappy," he says.

"What flavor do you want?" Nancy asks.

He hands her a five. "Get me a pack of cigarettes."

Nancy nudges me and I open the door, which squeaks and catches till I push hard. We both run inside. "Ugh," I say. The only flavors are Coke and lime. Nancy happily and expertly mixes the two flavors into a big waxed cup. I get a small cup of lime.

At the counter Nancy says, "And a pack of Larks."

"I can't sell you cigarettes," the clerk says.

"Oh, come on, it's for him." She points to Mike. There are so many love bugs splattered on Mike's windshield that you can hardly see him through the glass.

"Sure," the clerk says.

Nancy begins gesturing towards Mike, shrugging and pointing at the clerk. I can practically hear Mike sigh as he gets out of the car. The clerk looks him up and down. He is still wearing his breeches and his good black boots, though he has changed from his white shirt into a navy polo. A new cigarette is between his teeth.

"Pack of Larks," he says.

"How was I supposed to know they weren't for her?" the clerk says, searching under the counter for Larks.

"She smokes," Mike says, reaching for his wallet. At the last minute Nancy grabs a bag of Sugar Babies and slaps them onto the counter.

IMPOSSIBLE WITH NANCY

Mike pays for everything and Nancy keeps the money he gave her before.

There are two men, long-haired, drinking cans of Busch beer in the black pick-up. I notice them staring at Nancy. Mike notices too.

"What did I tell you about wearing a bra?" he says as Nancy gets back into the car. "I don't want you bouncing around, do you hear?"

Nancy grins.

"It's not good for you, especially when you ride. You're going to sag down to here." His right hand cuts to his waist. He turns and backs out of the parking lot and pulls onto the road.

"They're not that big," Nancy says.

Mike looks down at her then back up at the road. "They're damn good for your age."

Somehow it's all right for Mike to talk like this. He's our teacher and the only man we know, other than our fathers, and they don't count.

"And don't tell your mother I said so."

"She'll tell everybody," I say.

Nancy jabs me hard with her elbow. "We were topless sunbathing," she suddenly declares.

"You were," Mike says, "but not Lucy."

"Yes, Lucy."

I don't contradict her. I'm praying the subject will drop before I get teased. I stare out the window, hoping they don't see me blushing.

"Did you sunbathe topless, Lucy?" Mike asks.

I look over at him. He's got his eye on the road, both hands on the wheel. Nancy is staring hard at me, jutting her jaw, opening her eyes wide, by which she means, Say yes or else.

"No," I answer.

"You're a good girl," Mike says and smiles.

"Lucy is a goody-goody," Nancy says, throwing herself back against the seat.

"Then why are you friends with me?"

"Oh, shut up."

"Girls, girls." Mike's voice is raspy. He reaches behind Nancy and tousles my hair. He laughs, a low smoker's laugh. "Girls, girls," he says softly, shaking his head. Suddenly Nancy pulls off her shirt and there she is, topless, sitting beside Mike.

"Nancy," I shout.

Mike does a double take then keeps on driving. He takes out a cigarette and lights it.

"Don't act as if you haven't seen them before," Nancy says.

"That's enough," Mike says. "Get dressed."

But Nancy just sits there. I am frozen against the door, staring straight ahead. We are coming up to a red light. The street is deserted.

Nancy is holding her t-shirt, balled up, between her knees. At the intersection Mike gently brings the car to a halt and pushes the gearshift up into park. He turns his whole body and leans against his door. He looks at Nancy. I look at him.

He is amused. I can tell by his eyes. He brings the cigarette to his mouth, takes a drag and blows smoke rings, which burst against Nancy's chest. He takes another drag, smiles, squints, takes careful aim, and rings her left nipple, three times in a row.

The whole time Nancy is perfectly still.

"The light is green," I say, pointing. One car has crossed through the intersection. Another, I look back, is almost on top of us.

"Okay," Mike says. "Put your shirt back on. We're going to be late for dinner."

He shifts his weight and puts the car back into gear. Nancy lifts her shirt, looks to make sure the tag will be in back then pops it over her head.

When we pull up to the house, Dr. Meyer comes out and puts his arm around Mike. "Stay for dinner," he says. A few minutes later, Mrs. Meyer calls us. She puts the food on the table, brown rice, squash casserole, and a platter piled with roasted Cornish game hens.

Dr. Meyer is in a good mood. He's been up in his glider. He describes the sight of town from above, the excellent air drafts, how he floated for miles. He looks straight at me and says, "Lucy, I'm going to take you up."

Jimmy, Nancy's brother, says, "Lucy's the only one in the family who hasn't been up."

My eyes sting with tears but I manage to hold them back. I don't know if I want to be part of this family. I look up at Nancy and she is smiling. She is my only true friend. Of that I am certain.

Later that night, from the study, where I call my mother to come get me, I see Mike and Nancy walking down to the lake, though Mike said good night and supposedly went home. He and Nancy are shadows from this distance but I am sure it is them. Mike is holding Nancy's hand and leading her to the water. The black swans rise and waddle to the edge of their pen. Nancy reaches up and Mike kisses her. They wade into the lake. I watch them as if it's the last time I'll see them, as if they are about to drown. They drift close to the island where the alligators live and finally their dark shapes fade into the larger darkness, and it doesn't matter how hard I squint or stare, I can't see them anymore, they are gone.

PARADISE

Lydia and I lay on our stomachs in the back yard, wearing only the bottoms of our bathing suits. We were drinking beer and discussing plans for the garden. Lydia drew pictures of eggplants, tomatoes and corn on a piece of graph paper. In three days her husband was arriving from Ecuador, and Lydia thought the garden would be a good initial project, a way to smooth his transition from Quito to California.

"If this weather keeps up," I said, though I knew nothing about gardening, "it'll be bad for planting." I tickled Lydia's back and touched her neck underneath her hair, where she was sweating. It was early spring and exceptionally hot.

She stretched her arms, suddenly unconcerned, and lay face down on the page of a book she'd been studying, about a man in Scotland who grew giant vegetables—tomatoes the size of pumpkins, pumpkins the size of cars. Lydia wanted to copy his method and see if it worked on flowers. "We'll grow marigolds as big as people," she said. "They'll come alive at night and dance under the windows."

We'd been talking about the garden since August, when Lydia had returned from her junior year abroad. It had taken her a few weeks to tell me she'd married Javier, and she'd always been vague about why she'd left him in Quito. His brother had been sick; there were problems with immigration; he needed to complete a course at the university. At times I doubted his existence, though Lydia called him once a month and received letters with Ecuadoran postmarks.

"Do you really think he'll like it here?" I asked, remembering my first impression of Santa Cruz, when I'd arrived as a student six years earlier—the costume parties with punch bowls of Electric Koolaid and people dressed in cellophane.

"He'll love it," she said. "He's an adventurer."

"I'd be homesick."

"It's been so long." She scribbled a portrait of a man with long hair. "I can hardly remember what he looks like."

I told myself there was no reason to dread his arrival, but the closer it got, the more erratic my life became. One minute I was excited and full of plans—I wanted to buy a motorcycle or take an acting class. The next minute I was depressed, half-asleep on the sofa, watching hours of soap operas.

Maybe I'd stayed in Santa Cruz too long. Lydia talked about how beautiful it was, which only irritated me further. I considered moving to San Francisco, but the idea made Lydia sullen. How would she find a new roommate, a bowling partner for Tuesday nights, someone to go horseback riding with?

"But soon you'll have Javier," I told her.

I finished the warm beer and rested my forehead against her shoulder. Her skin was the color of ash but over the summer it would darken and she would become even more striking. People wouldn't know what she was—black or Indian or some strange combination. Sometimes I was envious and wanted to be as beautiful. "Oh, look at you," she would cry, touching my hair or my cheek. "You're much prettier than me." But she had ceased long ago to see any of my flaws.

"Javier is going to adore you," she said. Underneath the pictures of giant eggplants and marigolds she drew three stick figures connected by the arms. "We'll have big dinners and harvest vegetables."

PARADISE

I closed my eyes and felt the sun, much warmer than it usually was in March. Lydia rose and walked to the proposed site of the garden, matted with straw-colored weeds. She squatted and poked her fingers into the ground, and I began to believe, after all the talk, that we were really going to have a garden. I hoped we could make it a success, produce vegetables—corn and zucchini, tomatoes and asparagus—to feed us at every meal, even with Javier's extra mouth.

✢ ✢ ✢

The night before Javier's arrival, Lydia and I went dancing at the Catalyst, which was filled with regulars—bikers, druggies, and university professors on the prowl. Lydia drank tequila and I bought a Thai stick. We smoked it in the bathroom, crammed into the stall. The door was covered with dozens of men's phone numbers.

Two hits were enough. I spit on my fingers and pinched out the joint just as the outer bathroom door opened. Lydia was squatting on top of the toilet so if someone looked under the stall, they would see only one set of feet.

A woman began talking. "The guy is a pervert," she said, her voice high-pitched with outrage. "He wants me to make love to his wife. He wants to watch."

It was hard to stay quiet. Lydia's eyes filled with tears—from the need to cough and maybe to laugh.

"It smells in here," said another woman. "Someone's been smoking good weed."

I leaned over to Lydia. "I'll flush the toilet and you go out first."

One of the women turned on the faucet. The first one said, "What do you think? Should I make love to his wife?"

"Is she pretty?"

"No," said the woman. "She's fat."

Lydia looked horrified and I sputtered with laughter. At the same time my hand pushed down on the handle of the toilet. Lydia jumped from the seat and unlatched the door. I followed her out of the stall.

The women, their backs to us, watched us in the mirror. We walked quickly past them without saying a word. Outside the bathroom we leaned against a wall and laughed and watched people on the dance floor.

"What is Javier going to think of all this?" I asked. There were cosmic dancers who floated and fluttered with no regard for the beat, punks jumping straight up and down, redneck men pumping their hips and guzzling beer. We watched the woman guitarist, who sang a line and jerked her neck with such violence that I imagined her head spinning off into the crowd.

Lydia wore a sleeveless black leotard and a long transparent skirt. We started dancing and I squeezed her fingers and pressed my shoulder to hers and reminded her that this was our last night together before Javier came. I wanted to whisper some compliment—how pretty she looked, how I would miss her—but before I could say anything, she yanked her hand away and pushed me so hard I nearly lost my balance.

I stopped dancing. Lydia stared at the stage with fury. I looked up too, as if that's where her anger came from. I didn't know what to say. My first reaction was to pretend nothing had happened, close my eyes and dance again. The music was a big machine, screeching and pounding its cylinders.

PARADISE

When I opened my eyes, Lydia was gone. I finally found her at the bar, her hand in the back pocket of a man sitting on a stool.

"She ate the worm," the man said, holding an empty bottle of mescal. "She didn't just swallow it," he added respectfully. "She actually chewed it up."

"Something you learned in Ecuador?" I asked.

For an answer, she gave the man a long kiss with her mouth open. As I watched, certain details stood out—a few small white bumps around her lips, the pearl that was working its way out of her earlobe, a half-moon of sweat staining the leotard under her arm.

Abruptly she pulled away from him. "Hey," the man said, more bewildered than angry. He clutched at her skirt as if he were going to rip the delicate material gathered at her waist. She picked his hand off like a piece of lint. I followed her out the door. She was drunk and quiet as I drove us home.

By the time I locked the front door behind us, she had already passed out in her clothes. The next morning she got up, gave me several sheepish looks, took four aspirin and drove ninety miles to the airport in San Francisco, arriving just in time to meet the noon flight from Ecuador.

✧ ✧ ✧

Javier arrived with an old-fashioned trunk and he wore traditional Ecuadoran clothes—black cotton pants and a bright woven poncho that would later lay on the floor of their bedroom. He was shorter than Lydia and wore a gold hoop in his ear. His nose was flat and hooked like an Incan's. He had beautiful long curly hair and his English was perfect. He wasn't at all what I'd expected.

In the evenings he stayed downstairs writing poetry and sometimes we heard him reciting Baudelaire in French. He loved going to the boardwalk and riding the bumper cars, though he always got turned around and everyone rammed him. He was one of the few people I knew who loved both the roller coaster *and* the Ferris wheel. Lydia and I hated the Ferris wheel, so Javier went alone and returned especially thrilled after having been stuck at the top. "I saw the Dream Inn," he said, rapturous, "and Seal Rock and the lights of the cement factory in Davenport."

He was so fragile and soft-spoken that I was shocked one night when Lydia yelled at him. He'd only been in the country for a week. "You spent all this money on clams?" she cried, reading the price on the brown paper bag. Javier stood next to the pot, steam rising behind him. "Don't you pay any attention to the *price* of things?" She crushed the bag close to his face. It made a noise like an explosion.

"Lydia," I said, trying to calm her. She turned on me, flung the bag at my feet and stalked out of the kitchen.

"They are beginning to pop open," Javier said softly. "Come and look."

He picked a clam up by its edge and laid it in my palm. It was so hot I bounced it from one hand to the other. "Try it," he said and I tugged at the flesh, which was like soft rubber in my mouth.

"Oh, they're delicious," I said. "We should eat them like this, just plain."

"Maybe I will write a poem about clams," he said. "About buying a sack of clams from the fishermen on the wharf."

PARADISE

Downstairs Lydia turned up the music. I could hear the thump of her feet dancing in rage.

Javier dumped the clams into a ceramic bowl and called Lydia, who didn't come. He and I sat at the table, extracting the clams from their shells.

"Tomorrow I will search for banana leaves to wrap around tamales."

"Bananas don't grow here," I said.

"Maybe I can find them in San Francisco," he said, "in the market." I pictured him in his poncho, carrying a string bag and carefully selecting bunches of cilantro and hot peppers. I wanted to go with him and show him the bookstores and the bakery on 24th Street, where they made the best macaroons and *churros*.

"I was wondering," I said, "have you translated any of your poems?"

"They're very surreal," he said. He might have meant there were words in Spanish that had no translation, abstract words like "irony" or specific words for shells only found on the Galapagos Islands. "I could translate one for you perhaps," he added and rose to serve a green salad from a wooden bowl.

The music downstairs grew louder, as if Lydia wanted to drown out our voices. She was playing James Brown, the music she'd grown up with. Javier didn't seem to notice. He put his hand into the big pocket of his cotton shirt. "Dessert," he said, pulling out a speckled yellow papaya, which nearly burst when he touched it with the knife. Its black pellet seeds spilled onto the cutting board. He gave me half and stood for a moment, watching me eat.

Later he walked into my bedroom and looked at everything on my dresser, the clothes in my closet, the shoes hanging by their heels on the rack. He opened my drawers and touched my sweaters. I sat at the edge of the bed and thought of summer, of cold fog in the morning and heat each afternoon, of the two of them, lying still in the long curtains of August light, sweat dripping down their necks as they stared at the ceiling, just below my floor, where I lay waiting to hear them rustle and cry. Then I imagined them, still unsatisfied, softly calling up to me.

✢ ✢ ✢

"These are mutant vegetables," I said to Lydia, on my knees between the tomato vines. I showed her a green one shaped like a pear.

"That's a plum tomato," she said, digging moats around the flowers. She was about to set traps to kill the slugs.

"Do you really think we'll eat this stuff?" I asked.

"Look how tall the corn is."

The corn was growing fast, but I had ceased caring about it. The garden was Lydia's and Javier's now. Whenever I offered to weed or fertilize, they'd already done it.

Javier had gone to the store to buy sausages for our Sunday barbecue. Lydia's Argentine friends were joining us after their soccer game at the university. I stood and tiptoed around the plots of squash and out of the garden. From a distance, everything appeared to be thriving, with the exception of the flowers, ravaged by slugs.

Lydia's slug traps were elaborate—old margarine tubs buried carefully and camouflaged with fallen flowers and stems. She was determined to save the few remaining nasturtiums. I hated the slugs and didn't mind the thought of their shriveled bodies at the bottoms of the pits. But Javier couldn't stand it. He would rather have sacrificed the flowers.

"I like Javier," I said.

Lydia sat up on her knees and scratched her nose with the heel of her palm, trying not to get dirt all over her face. "Come here," she said. "Hurry. My nose is itching." She held up her dirty hands and stuck her nose towards me. I scratched around the sides, where her nostrils flared. She smiled at me strangely. "You really like him?" she asked.

For some reason it felt like a trick question. "Why wouldn't I?" I said.

"I think the two of you should sleep together," she said.

We were sitting across from each other in the dirt. I laughed nervously and waited for her to laugh, too. "That's ridiculous."

She forgot about the dirt on her hands and scratched her nose, leaving black smudges on her cheeks. "The funny thing is that I really wouldn't mind."

"He's your husband," I said.

Lydia shrugged and I stared at her.

"Isn't he?" I asked, incredulous.

"Of course," she said with an indifferent wave of her hand.

At that moment the Argentines arrived, noisy and sweaty. They were dressed in thrown-together uniforms—baggy gray gym shorts and t-shirts monogrammed at the boardwalk. I went into the house to wash up and discovered that Javier had been home all along, cooking *dulce de leche*. "Will you start the fire?" he asked and I wondered if he had known what Lydia and I were talking about, if the two of them had conspired. "Sure," I said, pretending nothing was wrong. The Argentines shouted for food and beer. They were excited from winning and they were breathing hard and tromping around on the deck. I lit the coals and stared quietly at the flames, barely visible in the afternoon light.

✢ ✢ ✢

I got a haircut, bought new underwear, and started shaving my legs every day. Afternoons, I would ride my bike to the pool and swim more than fifty laps.

Still, I wasn't ready when Javier crept into my room in the middle of the night, wearing a pair of jeans and no shirt, holding a bunch of pink sweet peas from the garden. He had written a poem for me, which he stood and recited:

> Across the caverns of stairways leading up to your room,
> I climb and like Orpheus,
> stop and turn back.
> My wife is in hell.
> She will always be there.
> But you, with your green feathered shoulders that flex like wings,
> your paper clip eyes
> wetting my cheeks with blood,
> You talk to me like a conch whistling ocean tunes.
> And I hear the small parrots
> that live inside your ears,
> the jungle of ganglia and vines,
> their damp nesting place.

He remained standing for a moment and I didn't know what to say. "Does Lydia know where you are?" I whispered.

"She's sleeping."

PARADISE

I sat up and took off my t-shirt and underwear. He bent and kissed me. "The poem isn't finished," he whispered.

I pushed his hair out of his eyes. They stared back at me like a doll's—shiny, without depth. I remembered what I could of the poem—not the parts about me, but the line about leaving his wife in hell. I didn't know what was making him unfaithful, but I knew it had something to do with that line.

I lay on my back under the window and smelled the salt air. The waves pounded the beach. Somewhere beneath the ocean floor, plates of rock were moving. If Javier and I made love, there would be an earthquake. The neighborhood dogs would bark, car alarms would go off, dishes would fall from the cupboard shelves and Lydia would wake up.

Javier kissed me and pulled me onto the windowsill. The wind hit my back and I huddled against him. He held my waist and I leaned out, floating above the garden. The flowers were trembling from the wind or maybe from a small earthquake, a tremor so slight we couldn't even feel it.

I looked at Javier's face and pulled myself back into the room. "What's the matter?" I asked. "Is this making you sad?"

"I don't know where I am," he said and started to cry. I held him tightly. "This country is strange," he whispered, "and I'm going to die here."

"You'd better go back downstairs now," I said, though I wanted him to stay.

"It's not that I don't love Lydia," he continued, as if he hadn't heard me.

"Don't be afraid," I told him, though I thought he should be. Where did he think he would go when Lydia found out?

Then I realized it was *my* relationship with Lydia that was expendable. She would blame me and it would be I, not Javier, who would need to leave. They would get a new roommate who liked gardening and spoke Spanish—a third person to define them and look upon their soon-to-be-seamless marriage. No more bursts of rage or infidelity. I would pack their transgressions in a suitcase and take them with me when I left.

✧ ✧ ✧

I woke to the sound of splintering glass. It was still dark, still the same night, and outside Lydia stood in the driveway in her white nightgown. She had dragged out the box of bottles to be recycled, and she was hurling them, one by one, onto the concrete.

I lay down again, my heart beating fast. Up the street a dog barked. Another bottle shattered.

I knelt in front of the window and saw Lydia's arm rise, then fall with a crash. The glass flew in every direction, glittering. Her eyes were wide open, unprotected. Her feet were bare.

The neighbor's front porch light came on. I put on a t-shirt and ran down the stairs. On my way past their bedroom I called Javier, who didn't answer. Where had he gone? Had she already banished him from the house?

When I walked out the front door, Lydia held a bottle poised above her head. I got ready to duck. I wasn't sure if I was in danger. Lydia threw the bottle wildly, so that it skittered across the driveway without breaking, rolling till it bumped against her car's tire.

She leaned down to the box and picked up a wine bottle.

"Lydia," I said in as normal a voice as I could. "What are you doing?"

She hurled the bottle like a discus, spinning her body and releasing it so that it arced over the neighbor's car and fell, shattering onto the asphalt.

"Lydia, stop this."

Out of nowhere Javier appeared, running towards us up the street. His hair was wet and I knew he'd been swimming in the ocean. Both of them were crazy. Someone was going to call the police if we didn't all go back in the house and quiet down.

"Lydia," he said, approaching cautiously. "I did it. I jumped off the pier."

Lydia held a Budweiser bottle. She didn't take her eyes off Javier. "I did it for you," he said and reached out to put his hands on her face. Everything about her hung—her arms, the gown, even the expression on her face. Javier put his arms around her. His clothes were soaked. He left the wet imprint of his body on her nightgown.

I walked back to the garden and stepped over the flowers with their pitiful, slug-bitten leaves. I listened for the sound of more glass breaking, but instead heard the creak of the door—the two of them going back inside. Neither of them was thinking of me now. Javier was a stranger I had never kissed. Lydia was a crazy woman who had never been my friend. It made me want to pull up the plants by the roots. I reached down, furious, but instead of pulling, my fingers felt the waxy skin of a pepper, and I began searching for vegetables ready to harvest. I picked the biggest tomatoes, and a dozen mature ears of corn. There were plenty of small tender zucchini, enough for a feast.

I looked up at my bedroom window, dark except for the curtains being sucked in and out. I didn't want to ever go back into the house. I dropped a tomato and crushed it between my toes. The rest of the vegetables I piled by the back door, where Lydia would discover them in the morning, when she came out, still half asleep, to water the plants.

THIN AIR

The books you asked for fell into various categories—fiction, history and metaphysics—but all contained references to love. The footnotes of one book led you to others. You presented him with titles and he accepted each assignment without commenting upon your taste or raising an eyebrow at the voraciousness with which you read. Where did he look? Did he scrounge through the apartments of Manhattan collectors and scour the shelves of second-hand stores? There was no book you asked for that he couldn't find.

Each time you walked into the bookstore where he worked, shut the door firmly so that the string of sleigh bells chimed, walked down the two steps and stopped to browse at the counter of recommended paperbacks; each time you left 47th Street outside—the Hasidim with their diamonds, the bargain hunters pouring in and out of 47th Street Photo, the businessmen and women hurrying to and from appointments; each time you saw him standing at his desk, heard his voice—loud, New Yorky—calling out the names of books he was ordering, you wondered, What will he say to me today as he hands me the book, the impossible, obscure, out-of-print book that I, like a princess, have asked him to find?

The first time you came into the store was as a teenager visiting New York. You had found the store by accident, wandered in, bought a copy of *Leaves of Grass* and taken it across the street to a deli, where you'd sat in one of the back booths, drinking refills of coffee and reading "Song of Myself." Even after you moved to New York, found better bookstores with more organized shelves and computerized inventory, you still made the trip to midtown. You were fond of the dusty shelves, piled two books deep. It wasn't easy to find a book without asking for help. Once, when you were going on vacation to Egypt, you bought everything in the store by E. Wallis Budge. That's when he'd taken a second look at you.

His voice made him seem like a man of substance. It was loud—a trait you usually found annoying—and except for the volume, it duplicated, almost exactly, the voice of your previous lover. You remembered the day you had recognized the similarity. It was like hearing a ghost.

In an effort to be subtle, you rationed your visits. It took you months to feel that you knew him. You overheard phone conversations about sailing off Newport—did he have wealthy friends?—and about a trip to Jazz Fest in New Orleans. In his excitement, his voice rose and traveled into the back room where you were standing near the Henry James section. You stared down into a collection of essays, open at random, and pretended to read while you listened.

You came to know him without asking a direct personal question. And that's how you tried to let him know you—by the books you asked for, the bright scarves worn to catch his eye, the dangling earrings from Central America or the Middle East, the shoes, always fashionable yet sensible, like those of all New York women, even the way you paid for books, not with an American Express card, for example, but with cash. Sometimes you stuffed your backpack with things you might remove in front of him to get at your wallet: a book from Coliseum, to prove his wasn't the only bookstore in town, the latest copy of the *Nation* (how easy it was to display your political beliefs), a new pair of stockings or lipstick from Macy's—you weren't above erotic suggestion—and even once your passport, its leather cover finely creased from traveling.

Your greatest discovery came at the end of the summer. He was tan—from sailing, you presumed—and his dark hair had blonde streaks from the sun. You had just returned from vacation yourself, a brief tour of Mexico with a girlfriend. You were wearing a yellow cotton skirt with fringe along the hem and a pair of squeaky leather *huaraches* from Taxco. When you entered the store, you were sweating, despite your clothing, from a thirty-block walk down Broadway. Already a blister had formed on your heel.

He didn't look up when you entered the store. He stood at his desk. There were always circles under his eyes but that day they were deep and dark and you wondered if he'd had a particularly sleepless night, or if he'd stayed out late drinking. He was smiling when you walked in, but not at you. He was saying to someone on the other end of the line, "Funny you should mention that. I collect old editions of the *Arabian Nights*."

You smiled to yourself, trying to hide your excitement, and opened a book from the current paperback shelf. You immediately knew the importance of this discovery. More important than the fact that he liked jazz or sailing. Here, it seemed, was a key to his personality. Of course, you had guessed he must have been a collector. But up until now, you hadn't known of what.

Before he looked up and acknowledged your presence—or perhaps he had seen you walk into the store, could feel you staring, but wanted to give you the chance to observe him—you tried to incorporate this new information. You couldn't have asked for anything more perfect. He had read the thousand and one fantasies, ancient, erotic; not only read them, he owned them.

He looked up, smiled and raised his left forefinger. I have your book. He mouthed the words. You smiled and nodded, meaning you would wait. You imagined him inviting you for a cup of coffee at the deli across the street. Or asking you to stay past closing time: wait with him till the other clerks left, the two of you alone in the bookstore. "Downstairs," you wanted to ask, "I've always wondered, what do you keep downstairs?"

You dreamt that in the basement there was a printing press. He wore a printer's apron slathered in ink and could print any book you wanted. Perhaps he even lived downstairs, slept in a small wooden bed tucked into a nook, a hand-made quilt thrown over the top.

He smiled and hung up the phone. For a woman who had seduced, or tried to, most of her life, who hadn't hesitated to smile, plead, or take off her clothes, you couldn't think of anything to say. You thought about the men, strung like beads on a gold chain, and occasionally wondered, though briefly—it was frightening to look too closely at the past— when you would be forced to stop. Maybe never. Or maybe one day you would choose one man and allow love to deepen and attraction to mellow, even disappear for periods of time. That's what had happened to many of your friends, at least the ones who were married. You dismissed foolish theories, promoted by hastily-published paperbacks. The latest: that some women, particularly those lacking self-esteem, were addicted to love. You considered yourself more complex than that. There were no easy solutions—pop psychology, marriage, moving away from New York.

Him. The chances of him being suitable for you, of him being uninvolved, compatible, willing to fall in love, were remote. In a way, you didn't want to find out. You liked the dreams you had at night, the fantasies, the excruciatingly slow process of discovering him by indirect means. You were even willing to admit how pathetic it was—that he was the most exciting thing in your life. But you were loath to give him up. You weren't ready to find out he was living with someone or he was gay or, for any number of valid reasons, he just wasn't interested in you.

Remember when you had been a junior in college, working at a coffee shop on campus? Every day one of the assistant literature professors came in, ordered coffee, sat, often by himself, at a table near the window. He always carried his *Collected Poems of Yeats*. You found out he was a Resident Assistant at one of the dorms and one night you knocked on his door. What in the world had you expected? For him to smile, step aside, invite you to his bed? He had answered the door and said, with a frown, "I don't even know who you are." You had stood there, speechless. He hadn't even given you a chance to turn and run. He had shut the door in your face.

And last year at work: the man from circulation, ten years younger, who had passed by your desk every afternoon to collect new orders. You had left him a note, tucked in amongst the papers, to which he'd responded by taking you to his favorite club, where heavy metal music blasted from every corner and men wore fraternity t-shirts and held drinking contests. The two of you had stumbled back to your apartment, and in the morning the man had woken up, dressed hastily and left before you had even poured your coffee.

The *Arabian Nights*. While he talked on the phone about editions and translations, you wandered through the bookstore, looking for a copy. It wasn't under classics or the Middle East, mythology or medieval literature. What if you asked him to find you a copy? Each book he gave you was an offering of some sort, though you always gave him money in return. Some of the books had torn covers, others were in mint condition. If you asked him for a copy of the *Thousand and One Nights*, would he go downstairs, where he kept his collection, pick out his favorite, the oldest, most valuable? Would he put a marker at the beginning of his favorite story? Would you read it, knowing he had intended it for you? Or maybe somewhere inside the book there would be a message, to which you would have to respond correctly, as if you were taking a test.

"Here it is," he said and you turned and he was holding the book you'd requested—a difficult-to-find translation of *The Master and Margarita*. "Oh," he said, "let me look at one thing." He opened the front cover, took the pencil from behind his ear and erased the old price. He wrote down the new one and handed it to you. "Not too much, I hope."

"No. You could have charged more."

He smiled and his eyes, which were actually swollen, nearly disappeared between his lids. The fact that he wasn't a very attractive man didn't seem to make much difference. You followed him to his desk, squatted with your pack on the floor and looked for your wallet. When you found it, you handed him a twenty.

"Don't give up on the other books," he said, nodding reassuringly.

You opened the book it had taken him only a week to find and looked at the table of contents.

"I've never seen this edition before," he said, "with the cat on the cover. Isn't it great?"

The big black cat, holding a revolver in his paw, was garish. Nevertheless you said, "Yes, it's great."

You placed the book carefully in your pack and strapped it over your shoulders. You lingered beside his desk, not wanting to leave so quickly. It was mid-afternoon—it was best not to come late in the day or during lunch, the bookstore was too crowded—and only a few other people were in the store. Your heart was beating fast. You didn't know what to say, if you had the nerve to say anything at all. Except there was one question you longed to ask: Would you like to have a cup of coffee sometime?

You fingered a book on his desk, *The Secret Life of Walter Mitty*, a book you'd never read. Out of the corner of your eye you could see his hand—little sprouts of dark hair growing between the first set of knuckles and the second. He was holding a mechanical pencil, poised to write. You looked up and the way he was smiling made you pause, then blush. He seemed to find your attraction amusing, like an adult looking down on a seven-year-old's crush.

You were about to turn without thanking him—how else could you punish him for being amused at your expense?—when suddenly he looked straight into your eyes and said, "Isn't it amazing, how the world is changing?"

Your anger vanished and your worries, all of them, seemed like silly wastes of time. Obviously you had been mistaken. He hadn't been amused at your awkwardness. Perhaps he had even felt awkward himself, trying to start a conversation about something other than books.

"Yes," you said, "amazing."

"The Berlin Wall," he said, beginning to scribble. "All of a sudden it's falling."

You wanted to sit at the edge of his desk. Instead you kept touching the Walter Mitty book, opening the cover an inch or two and letting it slap back down. You were glad, at least, you'd kept up with current events. You tried to think of a clever response. The newspapers were filled, as always, with rhetoric. But lately, in some of the articles, there were anecdotes, images, that made you stop in wonder. Not the usual sentimental drivel, but words and events so powerful, so happy, that they had been left unadorned, to speak for themselves.

You thought of the way he'd been smiling to himself. Maybe he had relatives in Eastern Europe, or in some way these particular world events had personal meaning for him.

"I read the other day," you began, "about how the parents in Berlin woke their children up in the middle of the night and took them to see the wall being torn down." You had to catch your breath after such a long sentence. "Did your parents ever get you out of bed to see something or tell you some news?"

He frowned off into the distance. "Only bad news."

You were chattering but couldn't stop. Worse, you launched right into a lie. "When I was a kid," you said, "my parents came and got us out of bed to watch a turtle laying eggs on the beach." In reality, no one had woken you up, merely showed you the turtle's tracks the next morning. But you were so unhappy not to have been roused like your older brothers and sisters, that you revised the story so that you were in it.

"I was just a kid but I never forgot," you elaborated, though in a way, it was true. You had never forgotten, nor forgiven your parents for letting you sleep.

He was looking at you, puzzled, as if he didn't understand how the conversation had gone from the Berlin Wall to turtles. You shrugged and looked down, apologetic. His puzzled look was making your heart beat fast again. You wiped your palms against your skirt and lifted the heel of your shoe.

"Do you have a Band-Aid, by any chance?"

"I might," he said. "A blister?"

You nodded, happy your legs were tan. When you had been in Mexico, you had imagined him there: the two of you lying side by side on the beach or gazing at the horizon from the deck of a boat.

"I thought your shoes were new," he said. "I could hear them squeaking when you walked in."

You gave a little nervous laugh. It was wonderful, of course, that he'd heard the sound of your footsteps, looked down at your ankles, seen the fringe of your skirt brush against your calves. He opened a drawer on the right side of his desk and while he searched for a Band-Aid, you peered over discreetly. There were the usual drawer things—paper clips, pencils, scraps of paper inscribed with names and phone numbers. You felt frightened and thrilled, catching a glimpse of the contents of his desk, as if you were seeing him for the first time without his shirt. But there was danger, too—always the chance that you might come across evidence of a girlfriend.

The urge to ask him for coffee surfaced once again, as if only a bold move would stave off the inevitable—you discovering things about him you didn't want to know. He pushed a stack of papers aside, found a postcard, a black-and-white photograph of a woman you didn't recognize. He turned it and started reading the words on the back. You leaned and saw the row of X's at the bottom, so many kisses, a long-lost love buried amongst the papers in his desk. His expression became wistful. You remembered a line from Rilke:

> A woman so loved that from one lyre there came
> more lament than from all lamenting women...

Your previous lover had given you a book of Rilke poems, as if to prepare you for his departure. Rilke, the poet of unrequited love, who preferred pain and longing to fulfillment.

You wondered how you might phrase the question. Would he like to go have a cup of coffee? Not now? Maybe later, after he got off work? But if he had wanted to go out on a date, he would have asked by now. Perhaps he was shy. But how could a man like him be shy, with a voice that could boom through walls, a voice any opera singer would envy?

He buried the postcard and looked up. You had the feeling he wasn't seeing you but remembering the woman who had written the card. He frowned a little then said, "Band-Aid," and dove back into the drawer.

"I can buy some on the way home. Don't go to any trouble." You could have reached over and squeezed his arm. Suddenly you thought of kissing him, of coming around the side of the desk, standing close enough for him to feel your breath, an inch of space between the entire length of your bodies, the split second before your lips met, the kiss.

"Oh well," he said, giving up.

"Thanks anyway." Your voice, compared to his, was a whisper.

Now, you thought. Ask him for coffee. You stared, and listened to the other voice inside you—whiny, victimized—saying, Why isn't it proper for a woman to ask a man on a date? Why do women have to be passive and coy? But you knew the whining voice was wrong. You were free to ask him; he was free to accept.

"I hope you enjoy the book," he said.

THIN AIR

Now he was trying to get rid of you. At the cash register, an old man was ringing up purchases while a customer, a fat man with thin greasy hair, waited. In the back of the store, another man sat at a desk, looking through a pile of index cards. Why were there only men working in the store? How many times did women come in, lonely women who bought books they didn't need, who lingered, waiting to be asked for coffee?

The thought occurred to you, for no apparent reason, that this was your one and only chance. If you didn't act now, you were going to lose him.

He shut his desk drawer and put his hand on the black receiver of the telephone.

You realized, with a pang of fear, that you didn't know this man, just as you hadn't known the others—the assistant literature professor, the young clerk in the office. You asked yourself point blank: Were there times in your life when you were so unbearably lonely that you were driven to concoct an entire relationship out of thin air? You looked down at his hand, still resting on the phone. Images of your recent trip to Mexico flashed through your mind, the food you'd eaten, the beer you'd drunk, the men you'd tried to attract. Yes, in Mexico—everywhere!—you lusted after men you didn't know. On the street, in restaurants, even taxi drivers and store clerks. The Mexican men had noticed you and approached. It was easy to imagine what they saw—from a distance, a blonde American, alone, in her twenties. But as they got closer, they might have seen tiny wrinkles between the brows, a bleached mustache, rough skin a little loose across the throat. Nothing wrong with a woman well out of her twenties, they might have said to themselves. There might be money. Or experience.

"You are beautiful," the concierge at the four-star Mexico City hotel had said, "ripe like an avocado." Immediately you had pictured the fruit's tough outer skin and hidden your face with your hands. He'd hugged you and kissed the top of your head. "I've never known a woman who took such beautiful care of herself."

What a lie. Though he lived in the third world where few spent money on creams or dermatologists, where no one paid Korean women to shave the dead skin off the bottoms of their feet, he met pampered women every day.

You were filled with horror, remorse. You looked up from the desk and felt the urge grow stronger. Just a quick cup of coffee, across the street. If he said yes, you would stop asking him for books. You would read the recommended paperbacks. Or stop coming to the bookstore altogether, begin using the store near your apartment, or even the library. You wanted to tell him, Just coffee. That's all.

He was looking straight at you with a kind expression. "Is anything the matter?" he asked.

"I was in Mexico. It might have been something I ate."

"Would you like to sit down?" He pointed to a stuffed chair in the poetry room. "Maybe you'll feel better."

He held your elbow and guided you towards the chair. The instant he touched you, you felt soothed, as if you'd been given a drug. You took your pack off your shoulders and sat in the chair. He said, "Would you like some water?"

He brought a paper cone filled with water. The old man who had been at the cash register poked his head around the corner. The minute you looked up, he retreated. You drank all the water and said, "I've always wondered what's downstairs."

He stood, adjusting the poetry books on their shelves. Occasionally he took one down and put it back in alphabetical order. "Just a store room," he said. "Lots of boxes." He'd lowered his voice. Just a regular voice, after all.

You looked down at your gauzy yellow skirt. It was wrong, meant for a younger person. You straightened the skirt and crossed your legs, watching the fringe dangle. He turned and watched, too, but more out of a sense of politeness. His look was almost gentlemanly.

You thought of all the things you might have asked him. About sailing or the *Arabian Nights*; all the stories you'd wanted to tell him about yourself, even how you had wanted to kiss him. But you would have spoken in the past tense, as if your attraction had existed long ago, and now you were over it and the two of you were just friends. He might have said, "Why didn't you let me know? Why didn't you ask me out for coffee?"

You would have smiled and said, "I was foolish, wasn't I?"

THE MAN WITH POINTED EARS

My name is Sam Beauchamp and this is the story of an encounter I had with a man from outer space.

It took place not long after I had moved to New York. It was evening and I had been wandering down Columbus Avenue, occasionally stopping to look at window displays or browse in a store. At the corner of 70th Street, as I waited for the light to change, a man grabbed me by both arms. "Don't be afraid of me," he said.

"I'm not afraid of you." I backed away from him and walked quickly to the next block. When I was sure the man hadn't followed me—I didn't see him anywhere on the street—I began to calm down.

I had only looked at him briefly. But I remembered him well; at least, one aspect. His ears. The man had had pointed ears. This is the sort of thing you read in a science fiction novel or a comic book. But this time it was real.

Perhaps he hadn't been from outer space. He could have been a prankster out on a Saturday night, wearing a pair of false ears and scaring people. Or perhaps there was some sort of disease with pointed ears as a symptom. I couldn't remember if he had had other irregularities or deformities, because I had been fixated on his ears.

And his voice, distinctly saying, "Don't be afraid of me." In retrospect, the voice had had a certain sincerity, a poignancy, that made me uneasy. In fact, I believe it was what the man said, rather than how he looked, that had so unnerved me.

And like a fool, I had reacted with anger. I wished I hadn't hurried away, that I had looked at him more closely, that I had at least given him a smile, a bit of encouragement, or stopped and talked to him about his predicament.

Over the next few days, I thought about the man, not often, but every time I walked past the corner of 70th and Columbus, I looked for him. At first I didn't tell anyone about my encounter, but then, the next Friday, I had a date with Grace, a girl I'd met in line at Zabar's. Grace and I had been out on several dates, though we weren't getting along very well. It wasn't anything particular, we just weren't thrilled with each other and in the absence of the sort of excitement that keeps things moving, our relationship was probably going to fizzle out.

Grace and I were walking down Columbus, and without preparing her at all, I blurted out the story of what had happened between me and the pointy-eared man. Grace looked skeptical, then concerned. I had the odd urge to say, "Don't be afraid." Instead I laughed and shrugged the whole thing off.

She laughed too. "Maybe he *was* an alien," she said with a giggle. She didn't believe what she was saying; she was just joking around. "Or maybe he was the devil, coming to tempt you," she added.

This was a possibility I hadn't thought of. Probably only a religious person would have thought of a man with pointed ears as the devil. Somehow, though, it fit.

I took Grace by the elbow and led her back towards my apartment. As I said before, we weren't really getting along. Somehow, my telling her about the pointy-eared man had made matters worse. I didn't want to see her anymore and after that evening, I didn't call her.

THE MAN WITH POINTED EARS

✢ ✢ ✢

A few days later, my sister Rosemary phoned. She was a student at Columbia. She and I had never been close and I didn't see much of her in the city. She had her own set of friends with whom she went out to jazz clubs and dance clubs. As far as I could tell, she stayed out all night every Friday and Saturday. She was studying anthropology.

"How are things going?" she asked. Without waiting for an answer, she jumped right to the point. "Do you think Larry would be interested in a new client?"

Larry was my mother's second cousin, a talent agent. I was working as his assistant. It wasn't the career I would have chosen, but I had wanted to get away from home so badly that I'd jumped at the first job opportunity.

"I met this actor—" Rosemary continued.

"Don't tell me," I interrupted. "Tall, handsome. Rave reviews in the *Voice*, an off off Broadway production, quirky but his performance shone through."

"God, Sam, are you always so cynical?"

"You wouldn't believe how many of these guys there are wandering around New York. It's sad, actually. It's so random. Who makes it and who doesn't."

"Well, Maurice is different."

"Of course he's different. They're all different."

"Sam, why are you so hostile?"

Rosemary had read a bunch of pop psychology books and often fell into the jargon. I took a deep breath and apologized.

"I'll tell Larry about Maurice," I offered. "Or maybe he can just drop by when we're not busy. Who knows? Larry might fall in love with him."

"He's not gay," Rosemary said.

"Even better. Larry loves straight men."

"Does he love you?"

I had never understood why Rosemary and I didn't get along. Probably just garden-variety sibling rivalry. She thought I had mistreated her. I thought she was a brat. Still, there had been moments of big brotherly concern. But she was sharp-tongued, like Mother, and she instinctively knew a person's vulnerabilities.

We hung up and I felt immediately depressed, lonelier than before and sorry for myself. My first reaction was to want to fly back home, down to New Orleans, for a long weekend. There wasn't much work at the office, though Larry had gotten tickets to the opening of "Titanic." Broadway musicals made my legs cramp up. Either that or fall asleep.

It seemed, in the end, like too much trouble to leave town. Besides, since my encounter with the pointy-eared man, I had begun to look at myself differently.

I wondered if the pointy-eared man had followed me that night, if he had, for some reason, picked me out of the crowd. Perhaps the man had sensed some quality in me, a kind of susceptibility, an openness. Had he been trying to communicate? Or was I just a random choice, a chance encounter?

There was no way of knowing, but I began consciously to try and open myself to another encounter. Every time I passed the corner of 70th and Columbus, I looked for him. There was a store there that sold

THE MAN WITH POINTED EARS

Japanese cosmetics and I would loiter in front, gazing through the window at the combs and brushes. There were women in white lab coats who walked around behind the display case. I often saw them with jars or vials in their hands but I never once saw anyone enter the store or come out with a purchase.

After hanging out on the corner for a while, I usually went to my favorite coffee shop and had an espresso. I had picked up the habit of smoking again. I sat at the same table most evenings, smoking and reading the newspaper. I bought a notebook and kept a diary of my thoughts. Often I would start writing about one thing—an incident at work, fantasies about my next job—only to end up writing about the pointy-eared man. One night, I wrote a letter to an old college roommate and described the encounter. When I reread the letter, it didn't seem written by me. I tore it up and vowed not to think about the man, not to look for him, nor hang out on the corner anymore. I renewed the pledges I had made to myself when I'd first come to New York: to be more outgoing, to make friends, to take advantage of the culture.

At the opening of "Titanic," my legs cramped up *and* I fell asleep. Larry threatened to fire me. He wasn't a very good employer. He was unpredictable and when he drank, he became maudlin, reminiscing about his best and most prestigious client—Tennessee Williams.

Our current project was the promotion of a record put out by a former movie star. This movie star wasn't known for her voice. My job was to set up a party with the record label and make sure the press was there. The star herself was a household name though by now she was well past her prime. But she still looked young and she still had the wonderful figure that had made her famous.

Organizing a party involves a lot of prioritizing, juggling, last minute frantic phone calls. I was busy all week, working late, and life almost seemed normal. Every night after I got home, I was so exhausted, I lay down on the sofa in front of the television and watched the sports channel until I fell asleep.

The party was well attended and the star was thrilled and grateful to Larry. The next evening, Larry took me out for a drink to celebrate. I had two vodka and tonics and listened to him weep through the final sad days of Tennessee Williams' life. Afterwards, I walked home, happily enough, but as I approached the corner of 70th and Columbus, I thought again about the man with pointed ears. The street was nearly empty, many of the restaurants closed. Almost all the shops were closed too. All except for the store that sold Japanese cosmetics. It was, inexplicably, open.

Don't slow down, I told myself, but I did, in fact, slow down. There was a voice inside my head urging me to stop at the corner. I looked through the window at the women moving around in the room under the glossy lights, dressed in their white lab coats. They never seemed to notice me. But tonight one of them turned and watched me. She put down a jar she had been holding and walked towards the door. She opened it and said, "May I help you, sir?"

"No," I said, "not really."

"Would you like to come in and look around?"

I entered and she shut the door behind me. The shop was quiet and dark. The women moved noiselessly, sometimes disappearing behind a door that was camouflaged to look like part of the wall. I stared down into the display cases. The brushes and compacts and lipsticks were all in

THE MAN WITH POINTED EARS

neat orderly rows. Another display case held frosted glass pots of muds and creams. I wished I had someone to buy them for, they were so beautiful.

"Perhaps you would like a shave?" said the woman. "Or a facial? Very soothing." She waved her arm at a row of chairs hidden behind a large screen.

Without thinking, I said, "Yes, a shave."

She led me to the chair and as I sat, soft music began to play. "Close your eyes," she said and for a moment I resisted, thinking about how much the shave would cost. Then she put both hands softly against my cheeks and told me to relax. I heard the sound of running water and smelled eucalyptus and menthol. "Here's a warm towel," she said and suddenly I was enveloped in fresh minty smells and the hot towel was wrapped around my face.

I have never been shaved by another person. I must say, more than anything, I found it erotic. Erotic in the best sense of the word. There was a hint of danger—simply the fact of a strange woman holding a blade to my neck. And as she did so, a feeling of helplessness rushed through me, a vast and all-encompassing helplessness. My arms and legs felt heavy. The dark room made the whole activity seem furtive, illicit. The woman pulled the razor up my neck, down my chin, then up one cheek then the other. I opened my eyes and looked at her and it struck me that her face was perfect. Her skin was free of any sort of blemish. Not a hair was out of place. Her lipstick was smooth and even, her nostrils mere slits. Every hair of her eyebrows was arched in the same direction. I had never seen anyone so perfect, and it struck me that such perfection was just as freakish as a pair of pointed ears.

"I've been looking for someone," I said.

"Yes?"

"Someone I met on the corner out there. It must have been, oh, two weeks ago. An unusual person, with, well, strange-looking ears."

She smiled and gently wiped the shaving cream away from my nose and lips and neck. "You mean, pointed ears?"

"Yes," I said, sitting up. "Pointed ears. Exactly! You've seen him, haven't you? The man with pointed ears."

"No, I haven't seen anyone like that. But someone else was looking for him. One day a young man, similar to you, came in and asked Jo if she had ever seen a man with pointed ears. I remember because we all thought it was strange. The man was so excited."

"This young man. Who was he? Where did he live? How long ago was he here?"

"I don't know. It was, maybe, a month ago. I never saw him again."

"And you never saw the man with pointed ears?"

"No, never."

My face burned from the coolness of the menthol. I swung my legs around and got out of the chair. It's difficult to describe the kind of excitement I felt. I believed, all of a sudden, that I was part of something much larger than I was. I thought, for a moment, about this other young man. He, too, had felt this sense of importance—I was sure. What, I wondered, had happened to him?

"Wait," the woman said. "I'm not finished. Please, relax. You're nervous now."

"That's all right. I need to go. How much do I owe you?"

THE MAN WITH POINTED EARS

She took her time writing up the receipt. She appeared annoyed that I didn't want the full treatment. I paid the bill and left her a too-large tip. She looked at me with concern.

At the last minute I handed her one of my business cards. "If you see that young man again, or the man with pointed ears, please call me. Or better yet, just give them this card."

+ + +

I waited for the phone call. I was sure, somehow, that the Japanese cosmetic store was a magnet that attracted the man and his contacts. Both the young man and I had gone into the shop looking for him. And my original encounter had taken place just outside the shop. At the very least, there was something peculiar about that corner.

I didn't tell anyone about these events. No one would have believed me. I wanted desperately to talk to the other young man. The knowledge of his existence both frightened me and spurred me on. I realized that if I had never heard of him, I might have let the whole matter drop.

Instead, I doubled my efforts to come in contact again with the man with pointed ears. I spent more time on the streets, searching. Inside my apartment, I paced. At times I looked at my situation ironically. What if the man actually had been a prankster and had fooled both the other young man and me? The irony was that he would never know just how effective his little prank had been.

On the other hand, trying to convince myself that the pointy-eared man was a mere prankster was perhaps a way of distancing myself from the encounter. I was deep in the throes of obsession. And yet, the fact that I was aware of being obsessed didn't seem to matter.

The whole thing, though, was becoming exhausting. I felt as if I had been stumbling forward, a character in one of those strange computer games, opening doors, walking down passageways, without thinking about how to get back. And yet, there was an answer, somewhere, just as in those games, there was a golden prize, just as, in mythical journeys—after all the tests of courage had been passed—there was a reward.

I began to feel oddly resigned to my fate.

And then, it happened. The pointy-eared man. One night when I went out for my stroll, he was there, on the street, not at the corner of 70th and Columbus, but a block further north, at 71st. He was walking at a fast rate towards me, on the opposite side of the street. As I got closer, I saw him in detail, though I couldn't, in all honesty, see his ears. His hair, which seemed to have grown longer, was now covering the pointed tips.

I stepped out into the street. The traffic on Columbus was thick with speeding taxis. I wasn't going to be able to cross until the light changed. I looked at the crowd on the opposite sidewalk. I looked up and down, with a mounting sense of panic. The pointy-eared man! Where was he now? I had taken my eyes off him. He was gone!

Finally the light changed and I ran across the street, trying to spot the dark head, the hunched shoulders. The man with pointed ears was tall and should have been easy to spot. But he had disappeared, without a trace. I ran up first one block, then the next. He was gone, gone without seeing me, gone without our making contact again. I felt dizzy. I had to take a few steps away from the crowd, down the street. I sat on the first stoop I came to. My fingers were tingling and cold, yet I had broken out into a sweat. I felt strange and more than a little ridiculous.

THE MAN WITH POINTED EARS

Hordes of people were passing by, not ten feet from where I sat. No one seemed to notice me. A couple of people glanced my way but kept walking. What if I had been ill? Would anyone have helped me? It was more likely that I would have been robbed.

I hurried back to my apartment building, rushed up the stairs and sat, panting, on my sofa. I turned on the television and watched with absolutely no comprehension. I got up and went to the bathroom and looked at myself in the mirror, wild-eyed, cheeks flushed from the cold. I pulled my hair back and looked at one of my ears. I stared and thought, what a strange body part the ear is. I thought of how a man from outer space might view this malformed organ attached to the side of my head. There was something positively indecent about the ear, the way it lay exposed against the head, with all its strange channels and bumps of cartilage covered with pink skin. Nothing pretty about the ear, pointed or otherwise.

When the phone rang, I was afraid to answer it. After the fourth ring, I picked it up. "Oh, Rosemary," I said, relieved.

"Sam, are you busy? You're out of breath."

"I just walked in," I lied.

"Listen, I wanted to invite you to a party I'm having. Nothing fancy. Just a few people at the apartment on Saturday night. Do you have plans?"

"That's sweet, Rosemary. No, I'm not busy. I'd be glad to come." I felt, oddly, on the verge of tears. I would have liked to confess everything to Rosemary. Surely, my own sister would sympathize.

"You can bring someone if you like," she said.

"I don't know too many people," I admitted.

"Mother says I've been neglecting you. She's worried about you. She told me to try and include you sometimes."

I wanted to slam the phone down. Leave it to Rosemary to make an invitation to a party feel like a slap in the face. But instead of being angry, I was suddenly able to picture myself at her party. Her friends, chic teenage girls clad in black, would surround me. I would be charming, a New Yorker at last, and I would offer to introduce any aspiring actors to Larry. I would drop the name of the star with the wonderful figure, and tell a funny story about how one night a very odd thing had happened to me. I'd met a man with pointed ears. I would tell the story in a humorous way, yet add a touch of mystery. Everyone would listen to me, amused, and even at other parties, better parties, I could tell the story. People might think I was a little strange but at least I wouldn't be standing around without anything to say.

NIGHT GAMES

My mother is afraid to drive alone at night. She can't see very well in the dark. She owns a very dependable old diesel Mercedes, and nothing ever goes wrong. But she seems to know that something will happen—she'll have a blowout or the oil light will come on—when she's driving alone at night.

When my brother Richard has a night game, she calls and asks if I'll go with her. Usually I say no and she gets a ride with the coach's wife. This afternoon I say yes, because it's the district championship. It may be Richard's last game. He'll graduate from Frankland Prep in a couple of weeks and next year he'll move to New York City.

I hear the diesel engine long before my mother pulls up to my apartment complex. I've been waiting on the steps outside the office, petting Boots the cat, ignoring my neighbors as they come home from work. I know I'm a snob. I've lived in better cities like Paris and San Francisco. I don't like being back in Tampa, where my family has lived for five generations.

I'm glad we don't have far to drive. The team is playing at the home field. My mother doesn't like the Interstate because so many people tailgate, so we drive down Kennedy Boulevard and then take the back roads behind the airport, past the only large plots of undeveloped land in the city. I can hear the crickets chirping as the temperature drops. The air is not as muggy as usual.

When we arrive at the ballpark, the lights are turned on and my brother's team is on the field, practicing throws. A man sitting by the fence is selling tickets to the game. I suggest to my mother that we sneak around while he's busy with other customers but she acts horrified and insists upon paying.

We always sit on the top row of the bleachers. I've brought a paperback copy of *Don Quixote*, a sweater and a ratty jean jacket. It's cold for a spring evening.

My brother is the leadoff hitter. He never hits a home run but he's best at getting on base. He digs a hole with his back foot in the dirt beside the plate.

On the second pitch he grounds out to the short stop. "Oh no," my mother cries. Richard runs hard to first base but he's thrown out. He curses to himself and spits on the ground as he walks past the crowd.

The next boy I root for is Tony Nucio, the catcher. He's one of my brother's best friends. He looks professional in his uniform, short and stocky with a belly that hangs slightly over his belt. He hits a line drive past the third baseman and runs to first.

The first couple of innings move quickly. Our team goes ahead. All the parents in the bleachers are either gossiping with each other or following the game. The kids run back and forth from the concession stand with big bags of french fries.

A dirty kid in a baseball uniform, about nine years old with stick-out ears and black-rimmed glasses, runs up behind us. He's been playing with an imaginary team on an empty field, swinging his bat and running the bases. "Mom, gimme some money," he demands of the woman next to me. Everyone calls her Boosie. "Go ask your father," she says. He runs with gawky steps towards a man wearing a Mets cap, standing beside the chain link fence.

NIGHT GAMES

"He's cute," I say to Boosie because I like her. She is overweight but she has beautiful dark skin and she's always friendly to my mother. She is less affected than the other parents and she once wrote a novel that wasn't published.

A fly ball is hit to center field, where my brother takes a few side steps to place himself underneath it. "Catch it, catch it, catch it," my mother screams until the ball is caught. I stifle the urge to tell her to calm down.

Jets are taking off and landing regularly at the airport just a few miles away. There is a full moon, which gives the planes a metallic glow as they take off away from us. I watch the planes, pleased that they always climb safely off into the distance. I wonder when I'll go somewhere again.

Someone touches my arm. It's my father, who has just arrived. Like my mother, he comes to every game, but he's always late.

"Hi, Dad."

"Hey," he says, stopping behind the bleachers where my mother and I are sitting. My mother becomes quiet and does not turn around.

"How are you?"

"Oh, fine," he says. "What's the score?"

"Three to nothing. We're winning."

"Good."

"How are you?" I ask again.

"Fine. I'm fine," he says and moves away. There aren't many places left in the bleachers and I wonder where he'll sit. He stands beside the second row and talks to a woman I've never seen before. I can see the bald spot on his head.

More and more students have gathered near the dugout. They never sit in the bleachers which, by some unspoken code, are for parents only. I see some of my brother's friends: Spike, the football player who calls me "Eagle Eyes" because I can tell immediately when he's been smoking marijuana; Neil, the tall boy with liberal ideas, who always sides with me when we have political arguments at the kitchen table. Even though I like these boys, I don't belong near the dugout with them. I don't belong with the parents either. I'm more like my father, who comes to the games alone and doesn't talk to very many people. Most of the parents are my mother's friends.

I watch my father. He's dressed in a sports coat and a tie. He probably came straight from the University, where he teaches at the medical school. He seems relaxed but still awkward, standing beside the bleachers. I feel like it's my duty to go keep him company.

"I'm going to go talk to Dad," I tell my mother, turning away and hopping to the ground.

I walk up to him. I think of kissing him but I hold back. We have already said hello. To kiss him now would be too spontaneous for the tight boundaries around affection in our relationship.

Before I can speak, Tony Nucio catches a pitch and immediately throws to first base. The first baseman tags out the runner before he can get back to the bag. The kids around the dugout all look to see what the parents are madly cheering about.

"So what's new, Dad?" I ask when the noise dies.

"Oh, not much."

"I still haven't heard from graduate school," I say to make conversation. "It's driving me crazy."

"Chapel Hill?"

"No, UVA."

"Oh," he nods. "Well, you have to be patient."

Richard comes running up to us. "Will one of you get me a Coke?" he asks and without waiting for an answer, runs back to the dugout.

My father reaches into his pocket. "Do you have any money?" he asks.

"No."

He pulls out two quarters. "How's fifty cents?"

"Better give me seventy-five."

I like buying Cokes for Richard and going to the dugout. I'm proud to do him a small favor. I don't mind passing by all the groups of students, even though I notice that Spike and Neil don't look at me or say hello.

I stick my head through the gate and see Richard. "Great game," I say, handing him the Coke.

"Thanks."

As I walk away, I hear another boy ask Richard, "Who's that?" His voice sounds impressed and I smile. I notice several girls wearing jean jackets, like mine except newer. I try to be graceful when I hoist myself up onto the top row beside my mother.

I lean over to her. "Dad's such a tightwad," I whisper. "He wanted me to pay for Richard's Coke."

My mother purses her mouth and gives me a conspiratorial smile.

A tall, gray-haired man who looks older than most of the parents walks up behind us and puts his hand on my mother's back. "I hear Richard is going to Columbia," he says.

"Yes." My mother beams.

"Well, that's great," he says and pats my mother twice on the small of her back before he continues towards the dugout.

"Who was that?"

"The headmaster. Everybody hates him." She shivers and shakes her shoulders. "He had his hand on me," she says with a mixture of squeamishness and pleasure.

In the fifth inning, the game slows down. The pitcher from the other team keeps throwing to first base, stalling for time. Richard is kneeling with uncharacteristic patience in the batter's circle. I consider opening *Don Quixote*, which I read for the first time when I was a senior at Frankland Prep, but with the lights, the announcer, and all the parents talking and socializing, I can't read seriously. It's getting chillier and I'm smoking a lot of cigarettes. My fingertips are beginning to grow numb.

There are now at least fifty kids standing in groups by the dugout. When I went to school here five years ago, there weren't even fifty students in the graduating class. All of them were white, too. Now I see black kids, an Asian, and one boy who looks Indian. The Indian boy is lean and his blue jeans fit him just right around the hips. I wonder if he feels left out because of his brown skin. I wonder if any of the girls go out with him. If they don't, I think, they're stupid.

Last summer, when I first came back to Tampa after college, I spent the night with one of my brother's friends. I had never slept with a boy so much younger. Steve was stocky and what I wanted to do was burrow my face into the meat of his shoulder. That's what attracted me to him. I met him at his house—his parents were out of town—and together we went swimming in the pool. Steve was shivering in the cold water while I floated in and out of his reach. When we got out, we sat on a chaise lounge together. We drank a bottle of Perrier Jouet champagne I'd brought with me.

Neither of us had a very good time. He turned over the champagne and apologized so many times I was embarrassed. Being the older, more experienced one, I thought I was supposed to teach him a trick or two, but that embarrassed me also. In the morning he wanted to have sex again. I just got out of bed.

I realize I've been staring at the Indian boy. I turn away from him and try to concentrate on the game.

"Does anybody ever hit a home run here?" I ask my mother. She seems not to have heard, but then she taps Mr. Hanson on the shoulder. He weighs at least 300 pounds. The wooden bleacher sags underneath him.

Mr. Hanson's son is approaching the plate. "No," Mr. Hanson says to my mother, "but you're about to see one."

The pitcher throws the ball and Mr. Hanson's son belts it. The ball flies further and further. It goes over the fence.

I am dumfounded. Mr. Hanson shakes the bleachers as he stands and cheers. "Mom," I say, incredulous. "Did you see that? I just asked you. Can you believe it? I can't believe it."

My mother nudges the fat in Mr. Hanson's shoulder. "Can you believe that?"

Mr. Hanson just claps his hands. A little later someone brings him the ball. He holds it up for me and my mother to see. "I can't believe it," I say.

Usually coincidences like this spook me but this time everyone seems so happy that I feel light-hearted.

My mother crawls down the rows of bleachers to go buy a cup of coffee. She and Boosie have been leaning over me, talking all through the game. Now Boosie is quiet. I can't think of anything to say to her.

When my mother returns, she sets the cup beside me and tries to climb up from the back. She can't hoist herself like I can. She throws her arms over the bench and puts both feet on the rail below. She just hangs there, her rear end sticking out. She giggles. "What do I do now?" she asks.

"Stop acting like a fool," I say angrily.

My mother immediately drops to the ground. Boosie turns to me and says, "You don't have to say things like that. You're not an adolescent anymore."

"But I am," I say apologetically.

I feel terrible. I've spoiled my mother's fun. I wish I'd kept my mouth shut. I've shown that I'm not as grown up as I seem.

My mother walks to the front of the bleachers and climbs up the rows. She sits quietly between Boosie and me. "Sorry," I say. Boosie pats her on the leg. We're all silent. Fortunately my brother comes to the plate and on the second pitch, makes a beautiful bunt.

"That was perfect," Boosie says. Everything blows over and my mother cheers again.

This will be my last game. The team will play next week and all the same people will be there. My mother will drive with the coach's wife. My father will go alone.

At the end of the seventh inning, the headmaster presents the team with their trophy. Mr. Hanson's son accepts it because of his home run. I move down to the chain link fence and stand with my father, watching through the metal diamonds. The lights make the oily skin on his nose and forehead shine.

"Would you like to go to the country club for brunch on Sunday?" he asks.

"Sure." It's rare for my father to invite me somewhere.

All the parents move to the dugout. Richard is trying to suppress a huge grin. He also accepts my father's invitation. He looks at me with lifted eyebrows, just as surprised.

"Hi, Eagle Eyes," says Spike.

I peer into his face. "You're clean," I pronounce.

Tony, Richard and I walk towards the parking lot. They both carry their jackets and gloves. I turn to Richard.

"Mugger in Manhattan," I cry, holding my hand like a gun pointed at his stomach. This is a game we've begun to play since he decided to go to Columbia.

"Watch this," he says to Tony. "Watch what I can do."

He grabs the lapel of my jacket, lifts me slightly, then shoves his foot behind my leg and throws me to the ground, holding tightly to break my fall. My glasses fly off the top of my head. "Watch it, watch it," I cry and Tony picks up the glasses.

I get up and wipe off my pants. In the distance I see my father walking alone towards his car. His head is down and his loafers kick up a little dust. His sports coat hangs loosely, as if he's recently lost some weight.

It's not that I want to run and catch up with him. I wonder what he's thinking about—maybe his wife, maybe dinner, maybe a patient at the medical school. What if one of his patients died today, I think. What if he lost someone?

I realize he didn't say goodbye. Maybe I should run up and tap him on the shoulder. If I did, would he smile and be pleased?

He walks directly to his car without looking back. My mother and I get into the Mercedes and soon I'm warm again, with my fingers in front of the heater. They tingle as if they've been dead and brought back to life. My mother lights a cigarette and slowly smoke fills the front of the car. For once I don't snap, "Would you crack the window, please?" I'm glad she doesn't have to be afraid, driving by herself all the way home.

A BUSINESS TRIP

I ran into Hugh O'Connor in one of the newsstands at the San Francisco airport. I recognized him by his profile. Even as a child, he had had a big nose and a weak chin, features I'd always found familiar, trustworthy. I hesitated. At that point it would have been possible to duck out of his sight. Then I said his name, and he turned and saw me.

"Nathaniel Jordan. Nate," he cried. He reached out and gave me a hug. He explained that he'd just driven up from Santa Clara and had some time to kill before his flight. "How about you?" he asked.

"I'm leaving for Tokyo in an hour," I said.

"I can't believe it." He pulled out his ticket and we both started laughing.

"Same flight." He was quite excited. "Isn't that a coincidence? Why don't we go make sure we can sit together?"

I'd been looking forward to twelve hours of reading, napping and writing notes. But I'm nervous about flying, especially over the ocean, and I was glad to have Hugh's company. He paid for his *Wall Street Journal* and we made our way out of the newsstand, passing through the metal detectors and entering the concourse that took us to our gate.

"What takes you to Japan?" Hugh asked.

"I'm writing a book about Japanese film making. I'm going to meet Akira Kurosawa."

"Never heard of him," Hugh said.

"He made the 'Seven Samurai'—"

"Is that Bruce Lee? I love Bruce Lee."

"No," I said quietly. "Bruce Lee was Chinese."

Hugh smiled and slapped me lightly on the arm with his folded newspaper. "Nate, I always thought you'd accomplish things. Writing a book, that's perfect."

"Why are you going to Japan?"

"Business," he answered. "Boring."

At the check-in counter, Hugh explained to the agent, "We're old high school buddies." He turned and grinned at me.

While we waited for our boarding call, we sat at a bar across from the gate. Hugh ordered a gin and tonic. I hadn't had a hard drink in years. I considered a club soda but instead asked the waitress for a beer.

"So," Hugh began, "are you married?"

He had asked this in front of the waitress, who smiled. I waited until she left. "No, I never even came close. How about you?"

He nodded and rolled his eyes. "Her family's incredibly rich."

Hugh and I had grown up in the same working class neighborhood and attended the same alternative high school in Brentwood, where the sons and daughters of celebrities went. Back then, we had hung around with kids whose parents had had vast quantities of money. We'd never had any ourselves.

"Naturally you married for love." I smiled.

"Actually she's a very sweet girl. Neurotic. Obsessed with having children. Unfortunately, we haven't had much success."

"I'm sorry."

"Oh, there's nothing wrong with me. And besides, I never really wanted kids. But Wynette is determined. It's a little frightening. She may well run through her inheritance at the infertility clinic. Now that would be something to be sorry about."

He laughed and ordered another drink. I was only halfway through my beer. Over the loudspeaker came the announcement that our flight was boarding. Hugh finished his drink in three gulps and we split the bill.

We boarded the plane and as we moved through the first class cabin, then business class, I thought it was odd that Hugh had a seat in coach. Why, with all that money, was he flying economy? He was walking ahead of me, scrunching his shoulders and holding his briefcase so that it didn't hit anyone's elbows. From behind, I noticed that his hair wasn't as neatly trimmed as it might have been.

"Here we are," he said, turning. "Thirty-one A and B. Do you mind if I take the window? I like to look out."

We took off and Hugh ordered another gin and tonic. An hour later, after he had finished his fifth drink, he nodded off. With his eyes closed and his mouth open—even, I noticed, a slight smile on his face—he looked like he didn't have a care in the world. The pilot came on and said he was expecting a little turbulence. Remarkably, Hugh didn't wake up during all the bumping and swaying. While I tried, in vain, to find a comfortable position in which to read or sleep, Hugh slumbered peacefully, for the next several hours, with his head resting against my shoulder.

✧ ✧ ✧

At Narita, we went through passport control. Hugh was red-eyed and rumpled-looking, his suit, even his face, wrinkled from heavy sleep.

The customs official stamped our passports without question. Hugh suggested we take the bus into town. Taxis were exorbitant, he said.

"Why throw money away? The bus is just as fast."

It took us more than an hour to get into town. We passed a number of lush green fields where men were speeding around in golf carts.

"That's my favorite thing to do when I come here," Hugh said. "The Japanese love golf. And baseball. If you get a chance, go see the Tokyo Giants. The vendors sell noodles. And the fans play drums."

For some reason, I didn't tell him that this was my fourth trip to Japan. When we arrived at the station, Hugh jotted down the name of his hotel on a scrap of blue envelope. I hesitated before giving him Sheila's number—Sheila was funny about her privacy. I told him I was staying with a friend. I gave him the number but not her name.

"I assumed you'd be staying in a hotel." He said this peevishly and stood there pouting. "Yes, well, you're lucky you have a friend, I suppose." Finally, he seemed to cheer up. He insisted I come by his hotel the next day for a drink. I said I'd give him a call.

"I won't take no for an answer," he said. "I want to show you the hidden Japan. I know the greatest sushi bar. You can't come to Japan and not go there."

"I appreciate it, Hugh, but there are a lot of films I have to see. I'll probably be at the archives in front of a screen till two or three every morning."

"Fun," he said sarcastically.

"It can be tedious," I agreed.

A BUSINESS TRIP

Finally, I told him I'd have a drink with him. We would have stood there and missed both our buses if I hadn't.

But I vowed not to let him corral me into some sort of sordid tour. Gambling, geishas, lavish feasts—all of it created to soak money from non-suspecting Westerners like Hugh. No thanks. I had developed, over the years, a great love for Japan, the kind of love you feel for a person remote from you, a person you couldn't ever have. Perhaps fascination was a better word. I liked to think that I had a unique perspective—that of the foreigner—and that I could see things the Japanese couldn't see, because they were too close. It wasn't that I didn't know about, or at least suspect the existence of, Hugh's so-called "hidden Japan," I just didn't want to go there.

Hugh clicked his tongue and sighed. "This is taking too long." He waved his hand frantically at a taxi on the other side of the road. Sensibly, the driver ignored him, unwilling to cross six lanes of traffic. Another taxi came along. "Can I drop you somewhere?" Hugh asked.

"No thanks." His hotel was actually quite close to Sheila's neighborhood but I'd had enough of Hugh for one day.

"Tomorrow," he said. "Don't let me down."

✢ ✢ ✢

Sheila wasn't home when I arrived but she'd left a key under a flower pot next to the back door. Inside her apartment, it was cool and dark. Immediately I felt at home. The apartment was sparsely decorated, the walls bare, and despite my fatigue, I felt exhilarated by the lack of clutter. It was the same sort of feeling I had after hiking, after being out in the wilderness for days, and finally coming home and getting into the shower, the hot water washing layers of dirt away in grimy streaks down the drain. I was stripped of my need for possessions, stripped of greed, stripped, almost, of my Americanness. It was worth getting that dirty, just to feel clean again. I put down my suitcase and took a deep breath. The air smelled faintly of incense.

I found a note from Sheila describing some of the food in her refrigerator (bread and cold cuts, a bowl of cherries). The note advised me to "sleep it off." She would be back after dinner.

After unpacking and taking a shower, I lay down on the futon in the guest room. The sheets were so crisp they might have been ironed. I was almost too excited to sleep. My entire stay was ahead of me. By the time I woke up, Sheila would be home. In two days I would meet the film maker I admired most in the world.

Just as I was drifting off, I remembered Hugh. In fact, I could hear his voice, calling my name. I was sure it was Hugh, really Hugh, not just my imagination. He was calling out "Nate" in a plaintive voice, as if he needed my help.

✣ ✣ ✣

I woke up at four in the morning, disoriented, then couldn't go back to sleep. I didn't want to go to the kitchen to make coffee for fear I'd wake Sheila. So I lay in bed until 6:30, going over my notes for the Kurosawa interview. By the time I got up, I had a headache.

Not long after I'd made coffee, Sheila emerged from the bedroom in a threadbare kimono. Her hair was mashed down on one side, as if she'd gone to sleep with it wet. "Nate," she said, smiling. I rose from the table and gave her a hug.

"I didn't have the heart to wake you," she said.

A BUSINESS TRIP

"I only meant to take a nap."

"Well, it's better this way. Now you're adjusted." She pulled the lapels of her kimono closer and cinched the belt more tightly. From underneath the cupboard, she retrieved a frying pan. "How about some eggs?"

"Sure."

She poured herself a cup of coffee and beat the eggs in a metal bowl. "So how was your flight?" she asked.

"Fine," I answered, not mentioning Hugh.

She brought two plates to the table. Along with the scrambled eggs was a slice of pale melon that tasted like cantaloupe. The eggs were sweet, scrambled with slices of banana.

"Thanks so much for putting me up," I said. "Again."

"It's nothing," she said. "I like the company."

If anyone had asked, I would have been hard-pressed to explain why I wasn't in love with Sheila. She was talented, smart, she even had money. She was half Japanese. It would have been convenient to fall in love with her. I had often imagined moving into her apartment, leaving San Francisco, leaving my comfortable and mildly boring existence, my friends who probably wouldn't have missed me anyway. To be honest, I was still hoping it would happen, that one night while lying beside her in bed, I would be struck, transformed. I knew that wasn't how most people fell in love but I thought maybe I was different. Maybe I needed more time.

After breakfast, we took a walk to one of the shrines near her house. There was a particularly lovely garden nearby, a favorite spot for Sunday strollers. People sat on benches, reading, or with their eyes closed, relaxing.

"You seem tired," Sheila said.

"I had a hard semester." When she took my hand, I instantly became aware that people in the park were staring. "I don't think I'm suited to teaching," I continued. "It was never what I thought I'd be doing."

"What did you think you'd be doing?" she asked.

It was odd that she'd forgotten this vital piece of information. More than once, I'd told her about wanting to be a film maker.

A light rain began to fall. Off in the distance—somewhere near Mount Fuji, I imagined—thunder came rumbling across the sky. There was something wonderful about a sudden summer storm, so unlike San Francisco, where it never rained during the summer and the hills around the city turned brown and the mornings were cold with fog.

When it started to pour, we shared my umbrella. Sheila reached up and put her hand on my face. She said, "You're always so distant when you arrive."

"I'm sorry, I don't mean to be."

On our way back to the apartment, we stopped at a little cafe and had two cups of weak coffee. The owner of the cafe and the other patrons ignored us. To my surprise, Sheila looked up and started to cry.

I hurriedly paid for the coffee and put my arm around her and guided her back out onto the sidewalk. Sometimes she was unhappy in this country. She'd been raised in California and the Japanese didn't treat her as one of them.

We walked up some stairs and started across a pedestrian bridge over a heavily trafficked road. In the middle, Sheila stopped and looked down at the cars speeding beneath us.

A BUSINESS TRIP

"Sheila, is something the matter?"

She stared down for a long time before looking up at me. "I've met someone," she said.

"You've met someone?" I managed.

She stepped away from me, out from under the umbrella. "I tried not to let it happen," she said. "I fought it."

I felt as if I'd been hit in the stomach. It was still raining hard. Sheila looked miserable, getting drenched.

We walked back to her apartment in silence. I had been so unprepared for her announcement that I could think of nothing to say. Sheila too seemed strangely unwilling to discuss the situation. She walked close to me again, sharing the umbrella. She didn't offer any information about the new person.

When we got back to her apartment, the first thing I did was call Hugh. He repeated his invitation for a drink. I told him I'd meet him in the lobby of his hotel. Sheila didn't ask where I was going and I didn't tell her. I put on my trench coat and started down the wet empty sidewalks that led to the Tokyo Prince.

✢ ✢ ✢

Hugh was lounging in a big comfortable chair in the lobby when I walked through the automatic doors. He looked as conspicuous as any tall blonde Westerner. He was wearing a beautiful linen suit the color of butter, which gave him the air of a colonialist.

"Nate." He held out his hand. "Get caught in a typhoon?" He laughed. "Let's start with a drink here."

The bar had a disinfected feel, all plastic, like a cafeteria. At the table, Hugh ordered a gin and tonic.

"Make it two," I said, though my stomach was empty. I reached into a bowl of shrimp crackers and dissolved them, one by one, in my mouth.

A Japanese man in a navy suit came to our table and in a thick accent, started talking to us in English. Periodically, he looked back to his own companions at a nearby table. I couldn't understand a word he was saying. Soon it became obvious he was plastered. I could have tried speaking to him in Japanese but didn't.

"Hey," Hugh shouted to the bartender. "A round of drinks for our friends."

"*Arigato*," they said all at once in drunken voices.

A few minutes later, the man in the navy suit, who had returned to his seat at the table, turned to a potted palm behind him, held his neck tie and threw up.

"Good Lord," Hugh said. I thought he would suggest we leave right away but he didn't make a move. The bartender, without so much as a sigh, picked up the plant and disappeared down the hall.

I stared at the group of men. "What's your business here?" I asked Hugh.

He didn't answer. He just shook his head.

The drunker I got, the worse my manners became. "Why won't you tell me?" I asked.

Hugh laughed and called for the check. We left the Prince, amid rollicking shouts of *arigato* from the men in the bar. The Ginza wasn't far and we walked towards it, taking small streets and back alleys filled with Mom and Pop restaurants.

A BUSINESS TRIP

"I don't understand. What's all this secrecy? Is it something illegal?" I asked.

Hugh grinned. "In here," he said. We ducked into a restaurant with the obligatory display of plastic food in the window, as well as the shiny plastic menu with pictures of house specialties. The prices were incredibly cheap. Hugh and I sat at a table. We ordered cold *soba* noodles, a light meal but one I nevertheless didn't think I had the appetite for.

But when the dish came, I found I was hungry and the noodles were delicious. I had new respect for Hugh.

"Good, isn't it?" he said, deftly shoveling with his chopsticks.

In Japanese, I praised the food to the woman serving us, which seemed to embarrass her. She hurried away. Perhaps I had broken some linguistic rule. My Japanese was crude but at the same time arch. I understood the language much better than I spoke it, a result of my having learned from movies. I had taken classes, of course, but being a writer, I had a near phobia of making grammatical errors. I would rather have not spoken at all than spoken like a four-year-old.

"What's your friend up to tonight?" Hugh asked.

"She's busy."

"Ah, it *is* a she."

I looked at Hugh. He was smiling in an unpleasant way. There was a bit of noodle stuck between his teeth. Suddenly it occurred to me that the "hidden Japan" Hugh had wanted to show me was the gay Japan.

My thoughts turned almost desperately to Sheila. I wondered what she was doing. I thought perhaps I ought to go back or call.

"Sheila is just a friend," I said. "Someone who puts me up."

"It's none of my business," Hugh replied.

"You seem curious."

"No," he insisted, laughing. "I couldn't care less."

By then we had finished our meal. I was sure Hugh was about to accuse me of being gay. I rose from the table. The woman who had served us, as well as the cook, came out and thanked us, bowing. I gave a slight nod and returned the thanks.

"I'm impressed," Hugh said. "Japanese is a difficult language."

We walked outside. The sun had set and the neon of the Ginza cast an orange glow all around us. The sky was still overcast, still threatening rain. Hugh pulled out a pack of cigarettes and lit one.

"Nate, you're upset about something. I can tell."

I shook my head. "I'm tired. I really ought to be getting back."

The narrow streets were crowded with people, mostly men. It was odd for a Sunday night. I had the feeling of being lost, though I would have been able to orient myself as soon as I found a main street.

"I've got to meet someone in a little while." Hugh took me by the elbow and led me, in the opposite direction from his hotel.

"Where are we going?" I asked.

"It won't take long," he said.

"Hugh, stop. I'm not going anywhere till you tell me what's going on."

"Don't you trust me?" he asked, flaring. "You've known me all my life. We were best friends."

I looked at him skeptically.

A BUSINESS TRIP

"I can't believe that you would accuse me of doing some thing illegal."

"What am I supposed to think?"

He turned and walked into the nearest bar. I felt dragged along, just as I'd felt most of the time in high school when I was with Hugh. We hadn't been best friends at all. Hugh was always swimming or playing tennis at the country club. He had gone out with the daughter of Eartha Kitt. Going out with a black girl, even one with a famous mother, had been utterly daring. No one, I don't think, had been Hugh's best friend. Or, perhaps, everyone had.

Inside the bar, he was already seated at a table in the corner. A small bottle of sake came and Hugh poured it into little cups. Normally, I hated sake but tonight the taste seemed muted. I began drinking in earnest.

"It's my own damn fault," I muttered. "For hanging around with you."

"What?" Hugh asked. "Nate, you're mumbling."

Music began to play and I looked up, startled. We were in a karaoke bar. A Japanese teenager climbed onto the stage and started to sing "Tie a Yellow Ribbon 'Round the Old Oak Tree."

"Jesus," Hugh said. "Karaoke."

"Let's get out of here," I said.

"Calm down," Hugh said. "We've got half a bottle of sake."

"I don't care." As Westerners, Hugh and I would soon become the focus of some heavy lobbying. "We can get more sake somewhere else."

Hugh smiled and clapped at the end of the song, the lyrics of which had been unintelligible. Some young people approached our table. To my surprise, it didn't take much prompting to get Hugh up on stage. He chose "Misty" and sang it well, not just on key but with feeling. I got up and left the bar.

Outside, I stood watching crowds of drunken men. It seemed like some sort of festival was going on. The air was so humid it was hard to breathe. Down the street, I recognized the group of men who had been drinking in the bar at the Tokyo Prince. The man in the navy suit, the one who had thrown up, was no longer with them. Somehow I knew they were heading for the karaoke bar.

They stopped in front of me, all four of them, and broke into grins. I smiled back and bowed my head in greeting to each one. We were fast friends now. They invited me back into the bar. In Japanese, I told them I couldn't sing.

"That's okay," they answered. "It doesn't matter if you can't sing. Let us buy you sake," they added. "It will help."

I followed them through the doorway. Hugh was sitting at the table again, flushed from his singing. The group of Japanese businessmen pulled up chairs and crowded around the little table, grabbing the sake bottle, pouring it for us. I wondered if the Japanese had an equivalent of the expression, If you can't beat 'em, join 'em. Several of the men, laughing, pushed me up onto the stage. This was not the sort of thing a grown man should do, a university professor, an interviewer of Kurosawa. The crowd chose a song for me, a ridiculous selection, "Proud Mary." Some people joined in on the chorus.

A BUSINESS TRIP

When I sat down, it was to much applause. My hands were shaking but I quickly drank more sake. Hugh patted me on the shoulder. "You're a sport," he said.

"What next?" I asked.

"It's time," Hugh said.

I didn't care anymore where we were going or what was going to happen to us. We walked out of the bar and down an alley. The restaurants were closed but there were some late night stands still open. Everyone was drunk. The streets smelled of vomit. The sake was like vinegar in my stomach, fermenting.

We entered a smoky bar. I settled onto a stool and watched the crowd, mostly men, but also a few heavily made up women. Everyone looked much younger than Hugh and I. What struck me was that many of the young men had bad complexions. The place felt unclean.

"Hugh." I turned to see Hugh walking out the door. I watched for a while, waiting for him to come back, then asked the bartender for a glass of water.

Someone leaned up against me, a young thin Japanese man whose clothes looked painfully tight. When I looked at him, he grinned. His teeth were yellow.

"What the hell do you want?" I asked in English.

He looked down bashfully.

I stood, tall as a giant, a head above everyone else in the bar. The crowd parted for me as I walked towards the door. The young man was following. "Goodbye," I said to him in English.

Outside, Hugh was in earnest conversation with a Japanese man. I stood at a distance watching them. At one point Hugh reached over and gripped the man's arm. Money was exchanged. I chose a street and began to walk. I looked over my shoulder several times to make sure I wasn't being followed.

I hadn't gotten very far before I heard someone cry out. At first I didn't think it was Hugh; it sounded more like a woman. Then I realized it didn't matter who was calling for help.

By the time I got back to the alley, Hugh was on the ground and the man who had taken his money was kicking him in the stomach. He was so busy kicking, he didn't see me coming. I sucker punched him, once. That was all it took. He fell to the ground, holding the side of his face.

"Come on." I dragged Hugh up. "Are you all right?"

He was doubled over and didn't want to cooperate. "Come on," I said angrily. His lip was split and his left eye was starting to swell. "Where the hell are we?" I shook him. He wouldn't answer. "Hugh, how do we get out of here?"

"This way." He pointed down the street.

I put my arm around his waist and dragged him around the corner. Naturally, it was hard to get a taxi. Drivers slowed, saw us, then sped away. I had to bribe the driver who finally stopped. The whole way home he watched us warily through the rear view mirror.

In the hotel lobby, every bell hop and reservation clerk ignored us. The other guests didn't look our way. In the elevator, I asked Hugh, "Why was that guy hitting you?"

A BUSINESS TRIP

Hugh wouldn't answer. I shook my head in disgust. I probably should have called the hotel doctor to come and examine Hugh. But I left him in his room, lying on one of the single beds, his beautiful linen suit splattered with blood.

A taxi took me back to Sheila's. I opened the front door as quietly as I could. My footsteps echoed and I stopped to take off my shoes. At any moment, I expected Sheila to appear in her old kimono. But when I peeked into her bedroom, her bed was empty and I realized she wasn't spending the night at home. She was with the new person, at his house. I went into the bathroom and washed off, then into the guest room and took off my clothes. I lay down, sick, full of self-pity. Somehow, I knew that what was happening to me was exactly what I deserved.

✣ ✣ ✣

In the morning I called the studio to confirm my interview with Kurosawa. His assistant told me Kurosawa was ill and had been taken to the hospital. My interview had been canceled. "I'm very sorry," she said, ending the conversation.

It was a little past nine. I made myself a cup of strong coffee and sat outside on the terrace. There was a haze across the city and the sun was a big orange ball, just like on the flag. What was the point, now, of my being in Japan? I thought about all the movies at the archives. I had no desire to see them. There were other things I could do: take the train to Kyoto to visit the shrines, take a bus up to the mountains, where it was cool and the hiking was good. Nothing appealed to me.

The phone rang and I rushed back inside to answer it. "Hello," I said, out of breath.

"Nate." It was Hugh. "Nate, I'm all right. I just wanted you to know."

"Thanks, Hugh."

"Nate, listen, I'd like to explain—"

I cut him off. "It's none of my business."

"It's not what you think."

"How do you know what I think? Anyway, it doesn't matter. I don't want to be involved."

"I took you to that sleazy bar," he said apologetically.

"Yes, well, you had that meeting."

"Maybe we could get together again?"

"No," I said. "I won't be here much longer."

We hung up and in the silence, I realized I'd been expecting him at least to thank me for stopping some guy from beating the shit out of him. Nope. Not Hugh.

I grabbed my coat and walked out the door. As I walked through the shopping district, I realized I needed to buy a present for Sheila. A gift to thank her for putting me up, a parting gift, something that would change her opinion of me, something that would make her regret her decision to dump me. Not an easy gift to find.

I passed the clothing boutiques and the shoe stores and turned down a side street and wandered until I found an antique shop. Inside it was dark and crowded with objects. As if to thwart people like me, there

A BUSINESS TRIP

were no price tags on anything. I hesitated to engage the store keeper, an old man who seemed both aloof and highly suspicious of me.

I stood in the middle of the floor and tried to look at every single item. I decided that when I saw something I wanted, I would simply to take it to the counter and pay for it, without even asking the price.

I probably picked the bowl because it was small. But I told myself that it was the most beautiful thing in the store, and it might have been. Needless to say, it was elegant. A red lacquered bowl whose sides rose like the petals of a flower on the verge of full bloom, like two hands cupping water. A bowl for holding sorrows and joys, or perhaps just for holding soup.

I reached for the bowl and out of the corner of my eye, I saw the old man move, as if he were about to rush over and prevent me from putting my grubby hands on it. But I was wrong. He had the decency to let me pick the bowl up and bring it to the counter.

He handled the bowl deftly but not especially gently. He wrapped it in tissue and put it in a plain cardboard box and tied the box with string so that it was easy to carry. I paid with a credit card and stuffed the receipt in my wallet, afraid to look at the amount.

Next, I took a train to the neighborhood where Sheila worked, in a section of Tokyo I hated, where all the buildings were large with plain impenetrable facades. Walking along, I felt like an ant. One building looked just like the next but finally, I found the one where Sheila worked and took the elevator to the eleventh floor. I asked the receptionist for Sheila. She said she was in class. I sat down to wait.

After nearly an hour, Sheila came out, looking surprised and embarrassed. She was talking to several Japanese men and for some reason I thought she had promised to have lunch with them.

"Nate," she said quietly, sitting down beside me.

"Sheila, there must be something I can do." The box containing the bowl was in my lap. Sheila paid no attention to it.

"No," she said, "I don't think there is."

I took her hand and held it tightly. For a long time I could think of nothing to say. "My interview with Kurosawa was canceled," I finally said.

"That's too bad. I'm sorry."

"I'll be out of your place this afternoon."

"You don't have to."

I stared at her.

"Where will you go?" she asked.

"I shouldn't have come here and upset you."

"It's okay," she said reassuringly.

"Well," I said, rising, clutching the box tightly. "I hope you're happy." It sounded more sarcastic than I'd meant it to.

She looked down and when she looked back up, there was something terrible in her expression. She was angry. It was a shock. I'd never seen her angry before and it occurred to me that that's why I'd failed to fall in love with her. I'd never had the privilege of seeing even the tiniest glimpse of her true self.

"You don't understand," I said. "I mean it."

"What kind of a person are you?" she finally asked.

A BUSINESS TRIP

"I don't know. You tell me." I really wanted her to. "What kind of person do you think I am?"

"I'm glad you're leaving," she said. "I really am. Even if there wasn't anybody else, I would want you to leave. I would."

This was more, I thought, than I deserved, but I didn't contradict her. She turned and walked back into her empty classroom. I didn't stop her to give her the gift. I just let her go.

✦ ✦ ✦

I started going to movies. I checked my luggage in a locker at a bus station and wandered through Tokyo. The only thing I carried with me was the box containing the bowl. Though I was tempted, I didn't once open it to look inside. I did, however, look at the receipt in my pocket and though the price didn't come as a complete shock, it was probably one of the reasons I decided not to stay in a hotel, even a cheap one.

I went to all kinds of theaters, big and small, opulent and crummy, in every neighborhood in Tokyo. At first, I saw only Japanese films, but then I started seeing anything that was playing. I was often the only Westerner in the audience, even at the latest Hollywood releases, including an Arnold Schwarzenegger that put me to sleep. I laughed again at "Tampopo" and "A Taxing Woman." I found a theater that specialized in fifties horror movies. I saw "Godzilla" twice. I even saw my favorites by Kurosawa: "Seven Samurai," "Rashomon," and "Throne of Blood." In between movies I walked around in a daze and ate noodles. When I got tired, I went back into a theater and slept. It was my own choice and I was, in a strange way, happy. Finally, after nearly forty-eight straight hours of movies, I retrieved my suitcases from the locker and took a bus back to Narita.

The flight back to San Francisco wasn't full. I found three seats, stretched out with a blanket, and told the flight attendant not to wake me. I slept deeply, without dreams, all the way back across the ocean.

When I woke, dazed, it was almost as if my trip to Japan hadn't happened. Even when I went through customs, no one stopped me or looked at me, much less bothered to search me or ask me about the bowl, which I didn't declare.

When I got back to my apartment, the first thing I did was clear off a shelf of books, making room for the bowl. There, it looked small and lonely and dazzling. It was lit from above, and the fiery red glaze seemed to be holding the reflection not of a light bulb, but of the sun itself.

THE BURGLARY

One night while I slept, a burglar broke into the house and stole the painting that had hung by the door. I woke in the morning and, as usual, got out of bed and walked to the front porch to retrieve the newspaper. My hand was at the door and I looked at the wall—it took me a moment to realize it was bare—then I imagined, quite clearly, that sometime during the night, someone had quietly opened the front door, slipped his arm inside and gently lifted the painting off its hook.

First of all, I was annoyed that that particular painting, of all the paintings I own, was the one to disappear. An oddly-shaped vertical landscape, it was a perfect fit for the narrow space between the window and the door. Every morning for six years, I had enjoyed pausing, just before going outside, to admire its strange yellow sky, the lone figure of a bare distant tree. Not only had it been one of my favorite paintings, but the artist had just died, causing its value to increase dramatically.

I am a collector of contemporary paintings. All my life, I have lived frugally and never traveled or eaten in restaurants, which is why I've been able to collect art. My collection is not important now, though one day, perhaps, it will be. When I die, the paintings will go to the city museum. When I informed the museum of my decision, they sent an appraiser to my house and he made his way politely through each room, studying each painting and taking notes. Later I got a letter from the director of the museum giving me a free lifetime membership and invitations to all openings, which I invariably decline.

Collecting is a hobby, not a passion, for me. It began almost by accident, one day many years ago, when I was walking past my neighbor's house and happened to glance into her garage. She was standing in front of an easel with a brush in her hand. I didn't, on that particular day, intrude, but I did stop one evening when she was sitting on her porch and mention that I'd noticed her studio out back.

She offered to show me her paintings. It was a stroke of luck, I later thought. She was an extraordinary painter, an Abstract Expressionist, a maverick tucked away in the suburbs. Like me, she had grown tired of her dark, cramped city apartment. She painted quietly in her garage and lived on her husband's life insurance, which she had invested wisely—surprising, considering her artistic temperament. Her husband had died in the war. At any rate, it was this neighbor, Mrs. Brody, who first sparked my interest not only in Abstract Expressionism but in collecting in general.

One summer day she convinced me to accompany her into the city, to a gallery that specialized in the *avant garde*. The strongest pieces in my collection are, without a doubt, the four Abstract Expressionists I've managed to obtain, among them a small, though representative, de Kooning. It was Mrs. Brody who had helped me find the de Kooning.

Even after she moved away, I continued to make regular forays into the gallery district, and still go, even now. "Ah, Mr. White," the gallery owners murmur, smiling, guiding me by the elbow into their offices. We flip through the canvases leaning against their walls. I always call ahead and tell them I'm coming. Occasionally they will call me about a painting they think I might want. Even in the eighties when the art market was booming, when paintings were being snatched up and large edition prints sold for hundreds of thousands, the galleries gave me a small courtesy discount.

THE BURGLARY

On the morning of my burglary, I made my usual mug of coffee and considered the facts. Somehow I knew, without making a thorough investigation, that the painting was the only object missing. The mystery was further deepened by the fact that the front door, and all the other doors, had remained locked. The windows were locked from the inside. The evidence pointed to someone in possession of a key but there was no one with a key except my housekeeper, Mrs. Jamison, who comes twice a week and would never, under any circumstances, steal a painting.

It wasn't difficult for me to decide against calling the police. In my experience, the police are meddlesome, loud, and have no tact. I have little faith in their abilities of detection and in this case, the chances of their retrieving my property were slim. The burglar, I didn't think, would try to resell. I believed, though I wasn't sure why, that either he had stolen the painting to hang on his own wall or he'd stolen it simply to bother me.

Now who would do that? I have no children and have never been married. My only brother died several years ago. Every Christmas I get a card from my niece with a picture of her and her children. No one visits and no one enters except Mrs. Jamison. Even the delivery boy from the supermarket rings the bell and leaves my box of groceries on the back steps.

After several minutes of thinking along these lines, I sat down at the breakfast table and tried to resume my daily routine. I read the newspaper, back to front. I ate a piece of toast with red currant jelly and drank my coffee. Afterwards, I washed the plate, knife and mug, dried them with a clean dish towel, and put them away. I tried to carry on as usual but because of the burglary somehow things had changed.

Every day I take a walk and once a week I ride the train into the city. The day of the burglary, a Tuesday, was not my day to go into the city, but I decided to go anyway. I showered and shaved and put on my gray suit, a white shirt and a red tie with small blue dots. I counted out enough quarters for a return trip, put them in my pocket and counted the bills in my money clip: sixty-seven dollars. I brushed my hair and finally, inspected myself in the mirror. There was a grease spot the size of a dime near the second button of my suit coat. I took the suit off and put on my navy one, folding the soiled one in a bundle to drop at the dry cleaner's.

Outside, the mailman shouted from across the street. "Hello, Mr. White. Would you like your mail?" He crossed the street but I told him I was on my way into the city and would prefer that he leave the mail in my box.

"I don't suppose you have anything urgent," he said and leafed through the envelopes, making a quick examination of return addresses.

"Just leave them in the box, please, as usual," I repeated and turned, walking briskly towards the train station.

When I approached the ticket counter, the ticket agent said, "Hello, Mr. White. A return to the city?"

"That's right."

"Why, it's Tuesday," the agent said with some surprise.

"Tuesday, the 22nd." I pointed to my watch.

"But you go into the city on Thursdays."

"That's correct," I said.

He smiled and handed me my ticket. "You have a nice day, sir."

THE BURGLARY

I waited patiently on the platform. As the train pulled into the station, I realized I was still carrying my gray suit under my arm, having forgotten to drop it off at the dry cleaner's. I could have retraced my steps, dropped off the suit and taken the next train. Instead, when the train halted, I hopped on, found a seat facing forward and set my bundle next to me.

The train ride into the city usually takes forty-five minutes. The day was already hot and the air conditioning on the train seemed to be working at less than full capacity. I pushed my hat back from my forehead and blotted the rim of perspiration with a handkerchief. The fact that I had forgotten to drop off my suit was causing me some anxiety. Not only do I rely on my memory; my memory is a source of pride. I take pleasure in defying the odds of old age. I have retained my independence and managed not to succumb to the false comforts of the weak and weak-minded: religion, pets, retirement communities and television.

But because of the stolen painting, I felt that my course had been altered, the very course of my life. I began to ask questions like, Was I on the right train? Had I brushed my teeth? I looked down at my ankles to make sure I had actually put on a matching pair of socks.

Finally the train pulled into the station. I walked through the underground walkway and up the stairs to the street. I decided to walk to the gallery district and try to find a replacement for the painting that had been stolen. With that in mind, I set off downtown, meanwhile keeping an eye out for a dry cleaner where I might drop off my suit. The city is set up in a grid, the streets and avenues all numbered. It's impossible to get lost, even if you wander around blindfolded. Nevertheless, after walking several blocks, I looked up and realized that the street numbers were going up rather than down. The traffic light turned green but I stood at the corner, staring up at the street sign.

I continued walking northward. It was as if my feet knew where to take me. It had become very hot. I was thirsty and looked around for a street vendor. I saw a red umbrella down the next street, which had the added advantage of being shaded from the sun by several tall buildings. The side street was less crowded than the avenue. I turned and headed towards the vendor.

The smell of hot dogs was overpowering. I bought a soda and gulped it so quickly, the vendor looked at me then looked away in what seemed to be studied avoidance. I started down the street, not towards the avenue from which I'd just come but in the opposite direction.

I came to a familiar door. After a moment I realized it was the entrance to St. Stephen's Episcopal Church, where my mother had taken me every Sunday when I was a child, as if to undo or counteract the Catholicism I got five days a week at school. I stared at the stained glass windows above the door, the same faded windows that had been there a half century ago, and took the last sip of my soda, which wasn't quenching my thirst, but was reviving me. I set the can down on the sidewalk, thinking I would pick it up on the way back out, and stepped through the doors.

The church was empty and cool. I took off my hat and held it in my hand as I wandered up the side aisle to the nave. I sat in the front pew, again placing my gray suit next to me. An elderly lady in a plain brown dress was cleaning the altar and setting vases of flowers on either side of the gold cross. The flowers were beautiful, cornflowers and daisies and black-eyed susans. In fact, every flower in the bunch was a wildflower. I wondered if the lady had picked them herself, in the park or along the side of a road.

She turned and smiled. I bowed my head, as if I were praying. It was the first time I could ever remember being inside a church and enjoying myself. There was no priest talking about things I didn't believe in, and no hypocrites enduring the Sunday service for appearance's sake.

Though I am not at all religious, I do have a strict moral code. For instance, I will not lie. I would rather not talk to a single soul than risk the possibility of lying. I worked for an honest wage until I retired. I have always tried to be generous with those I come in contact with, for instance, giving Christmas presents to Mrs. Jamison, the delivery boy and the mailman.

I stopped and wondered if I were speaking out loud. I discovered, to my astonishment, that the person to whom I was addressing this speech, a sort of apology for the way I'd lived, was none other than God. I looked up and the lady with the flowers was gone. I sat back against the wooden pew and stared at the crucifix, the altar of carved ivory, the green cloth indicating the season—was it Trinity?—and above, the silver organ pipes. I noticed something moving out of the corner of my eye. A roach had climbed up onto one of the hymnals and appeared to be chewing the frayed red corner. The roach paid no attention to me and went on chewing and moving its antennae. I made no move to frighten or kill it.

I was tired and despite the hard wooden pew, I was comfortable sitting there. I traced back the events of this unusual day, starting with the theft of my painting. I had liked the painting because it had reminded me of one of Mrs. Brody's, though, being a landscape, it had in no way resembled one of her abstracts except perhaps in color, that beautiful yellow sky. She had painted shapes, using a lot of yellow, which I knew, from collecting, was one of the most difficult colors to work with. She had tried several times to give me one of her paintings but I had always refused. Now that the landscape, the last faint reminder of her, was gone, I thought sadly, I might never be prompted to think of her again.

I remembered the day Mrs. Brody and I had come into the city and walked to the gallery district. That day, too, had been hot. Mrs. Brody had worn a fashionable blue hat and despite the heat, had remained admirably cool. She had spoken, with perfect politeness and obvious expertise, to each of the gallery owners. Suddenly I wondered if I had ever properly thanked her for all she had done. Somehow I felt I hadn't.

When I finally got up from the bench, the roach scurried down the front side of the pew. My knees were stiff and as I walked back down the aisle, my footsteps echoed against the marble. Beside the door, there were some flyers advertising a concert and a box for contributions. I reached into my pocket for my money clip and put a dollar into the box.

"Oh, thank you," a voice said, startling me. I looked around for the person who had spoken but the back of the church was dark and there were many hidden corners and small peculiar doorways. I found that I was trembling.

From out of the shadows, a figure appeared. It was the woman who had been fixing the flowers. "I'm sorry if I frightened you," she said.

"No, not at all." I wondered how long she had been watching me.

THE BURGLARY

She came closer and when her hand touched the sleeve of my suit coat, I didn't flinch or move away. "Are you all right?"

"Yes, perfectly."

"The church is a nice place to rest on a hot day," she said. She was not as old as I'd thought at first. Her hair was prematurely gray, I guessed, judging from her face, which was not at all wrinkled.

"I was remembering a friend of mine," I said.

I had no idea what had come over me to make me confide an intimate thought to a stranger, but I was actually leaning on her arm, as if I had suddenly grown weak and could no longer support myself. Though she was a slim woman, she seemed able to hold my weight without difficulty. She led me back to one of the pews and the two of us sat down. Her closeness was oddly comforting and before I knew it, I had rested my shoulder against hers.

Neither of us spoke. After a moment, I straightened and stood. "I'm fine now," I said.

She smiled and led me out of the pew. I let go of her arm and walked to the door. But when I turned to say good-bye, she had disappeared into the darkness or behind one of the peculiar doors, though I hadn't heard one open or close. I stood, peering into the darkness, seeing nothing, hearing no sound.

Outside, the sun was even hotter and the air almost too thick to breathe. From somewhere nearby came the sound of crickets, an odd sound for the middle of the city. I put my hat back on and tucked the suit under my arm. My soda can had disappeared from the step. There was a tremor in my hands and throughout my body and I knew it wasn't going to subside until I got home. It required great discipline for me to walk back to the station instead of returning to the church.

As I waited on the underground platform for the train, I remembered that at the end of that hot day of gallery shopping with Mrs. Brody, she and I had made our way back to the station to wait for the train. A man had approached, a wino with a nearly empty bottle in his hand, and I had moved to protect Mrs. Brody, under the impression that the wino was about to attack. She reached into her purse to give him a quarter, which he had begun to beg for in plaintive tones. I commanded her to put her quarter away. She gave me a look that even now fills me with dread. I held her by the wrist, preventing her by force from giving her quarter away. I can still see her rubbing the wrist I had held too tightly. She had too generous a heart, a heart that bled for every stray and passerby.

I rode the train home and walked down the sidewalk to my house, unlocking the front door and going inside. Just to make sure, I turned and looked at the wall. The painting was still missing but I could almost see its outline, probably because I had just come in from outside. Or maybe the memory of the painting was so strong that my eyes were making up for what wasn't there. I dropped the gray suit in a heap by the door and sat down, exhausted, in my recliner.

When I woke up, it was late afternoon. I heard the sound of a lawn mower. The house felt stifling with all the windows shut. I made a cup of tea and went out to the front porch.

I sat in one of the two Adirondack chairs and watched the neighborhood goings-on—the yard man mowing the lawn across the street, kids riding bikes, a cat running at break-neck speed down the sidewalk.

THE BURGLARY

Slowly darkness came. The street lights flickered then came on and the kids that had been playing in their yards went inside. It was past dinnertime but I wasn't hungry. My tea had long since grown cold. I sat on the porch, listening but hearing nothing out of the ordinary, till the lights in all the houses had gone off and another day had passed.

DEVOTION

One autumn night when my husband and I were driving home from dinner, we stopped in on the local high school football game. We had decided, after a careful discussion at dinner, that neither of us wanted children. This was a subject we had discussed before marrying, of course, but only superficially. Now the decision was more or less final and I think, in a way, we were both feeling sad, and that's why we stopped to watch the game. We didn't want to go straight home to our quiet house with only each other. We wanted to be in a crowd.

The lights, the band, the cheerleaders, the players—all brought out a weird excitement in me. I hadn't watched a football game in twenty years. My husband was astonished to discover that I knew many of the rules and strategies, and I told him a story about my childhood, a story I realized I'd been waiting to tell him.

I grew up in Tampa, at a time when the University still had its football team. I began going to games at a young age because it pleased my father. Then Lily, the girl down the street, joined us and for a number of years, football season was what Lily and I looked forward to most, the time of year when we started back to school and the boredom of summer ended and our lives once again had purpose.

The autumn when I was nine and Lily was eight, the University of Tampa Spartans were undefeated. The team hadn't had an easy season; however, the most difficult game was yet to be played: against the Miami Hurricanes. Lily and I had begged for weeks to be allowed to follow the team to Miami. Our parents said no. Then, for some reason, they changed their minds. My father was on call that weekend; Lily's father volunteered to take us.

At that age, I was, in some ways, naive, in other ways confident, savvy. My mother had led me to believe I was smart, though she said just as often I was selfish. I was a small, quiet girl with glasses who read a lot of Nancy Drew. So did Lily, of course. She and I did everything together except go to the same school. She went to Sacred Heart, a girls' school run by nuns, while I went to St. Bartholomew's Parish Day School, Episcopal and co-ed and overseen by a bald, pot-bellied headmaster.

Lily and I were good friends, equals, and we made decisions with the sort of fairness rare in children that age. This was surprising because we were otherwise so constrained—by our parents, who were not fun-loving or demonstrative, by our strict teachers who assigned hours of homework every night, and by the small Tampa society within which we lived, with its emphasis on manners, good behavior and obligation. There was only one place where we were allowed to be anything but perfect ladies, and that was at Spartan football games, where we were allowed to yell.

The 1966 Spartan team was the best ever to take the field. The quarterback that year was Freddie Isaiah, who would go on to play for the San Francisco Forty-Niners. Lily and I were terribly proud of Freddie. It made no difference to us that Freddie was the only black quarterback in college football. It was our parents who didn't like it. They said a black man didn't have the brains to lead a team.

As the big game approached, Lily and I began to pray. Lily went to the school chapel every day. I went to the big church at St. Bart's. We figured God would hear us because we were the only girls praying for a football team.

On the Friday before our flight to Miami, Lily and I were up in our attic, making plans. It was after school but before dinner and already dark outside. Lily and I had been discussing the airplane. She had never flown and I, who had once flown to Chicago, was telling her about the food, the neatly wrapped sandwich, the little square of cake, the utensils, the cup—everything fitted precisely to the dimensions of the plastic tray. Lily couldn't wait to try eating on a plane. I also explained to her what air pockets were, and when she made a face, I said it was like going fast over the "whee" bridge on Davis Islands and that seemed to reassure her.

I opened an old foot locker where we kept our Spartan scrapbook. Lily had brought up the collection of newspapers from the week, which contained more than the usual number of articles about the Spartans, as well as a pair of scissors and some glue. She cut and I pasted. We worked quietly, each absorbed in some private anticipation of the events of the next day. I brushed glue onto the back of an article about Freddie Isaiah's family—he had three younger brothers who planned to play football for the University of Tampa—but stopped for a moment. I heard a scratching sound.

"What's that noise?" I whispered and Lily stopped her cutting.

"Do you think it's a rat?" she asked. We were both afraid of rats.

Something kept us from running down the stairs. We listened more closely and the sound didn't exactly seem like scratching, more like rusty squeaking.

We held hands and followed the sound, leaving the safety of our little square of floor and venturing onto the rafters. In the corner of the attic dust seemed to be swirling. The blades of the attic fan were turning slowly, as if someone had recently cut off the switch.

Lily tightened her grip on my hand. I turned and saw what she saw. A vision. It was surely a vision. In the darkest corner of the attic there was a cluster of clouds, miniature clouds, white and billowy, the kind you see on a summer afternoon. I stared at the clouds and something convinced me that an angel was about to appear.

We watched in silence, waiting for a message, until finally the clouds started to break up. I looked at Lily and we both turned and stepped carefully back over the rafters. It wasn't as if we'd seen a ghost or anything to be frightened of. When we got down the stairs and into my bedroom, we agreed that it must have been a vision from God. We felt honored, singled out, like Moses.

"Could it have meant something about flying?" Lily speculated.

"I think it was heaven," I said.

"Do you think it means the Spartans will win?"

We believed our prayers had been answered.

The next day Mrs. Stewart drove us to the airport. My mother had given me explicit instructions about wearing my raincoat and using my umbrella. She had given me twenty dollars and told me to buy hot dogs for myself, Lily and Mr. Stewart. On the plane, Lily and I were disappointed because they didn't serve a meal. They did, however, pour us Cokes and hand us little packets of peanuts and at the end of the flight we were both presented with pins in the shape of wings.

DEVOTION

All during the flight, Mr. Stewart kept looking across our laps out the window. It had turned dark and rainy and the plane bounced around. "Air pockets," Lily whispered to me. Finally the ground appeared and the wheels of the plane touched the runway. We hurried through the terminal and Lily and I stood on the sidewalk outside the baggage claim area while Mr. Stewart went off to get the rental car. The rain blew onto our legs in gusts and we held our knapsacks and shivered, not daring to move from the spot where Mr. Stewart had left us.

"I don't know, girls," he said, hustling us into the car. He sat behind the steering wheel, looking at the sky. He consulted a crude one-page map of Miami. We sat there until the windows began to fog up and Mr. Stewart fumbled with the defroster, then started wiping the inside of the windshield with his hand. Even I knew that you didn't wipe the glass with your hand.

"Daddy," Lily said, "aren't we going to the game?"

"Be quiet, Lily. You girls just be quiet."

I said my prayers as Mr. Stewart nosed the car out into the storm. "God damn it," he said. "I can't see a God damn thing."

We sped along blindly, occasionally hitting a deep puddle, which caused us to slow and swerve and spray a great arc of water out over the curb. Mr. Stewart peered at street signs and hit the dashboard with the flat of his palm and cursed about being lost. I watched the road vigilantly, my eyes veering over to shapes as they loomed up out of the downpour. But nothing was recognizable and all of the signs and billboards seemed to be in Spanish.

"We're looking for the Tamiami Trail," Mr. Stewart said. "Look, girls," he commanded. Finally we pulled into the parking lot of a coffee shop. Lily said she had to go to the bathroom.

"Can't you wait?" Mr. Stewart said. "Come on, then. Both of you."

I reached into the back seat for my raincoat but Mr. Stewart said, "Just run. You won't get wet. We don't have time for all this." Lily and I dashed into the coffee shop behind Mr. Stewart, who held the door open for us. It was warm inside and there were pictures of the Virgin Mary on the walls and even a little shrine with lit candles by the cash register. Lily and I were both soaking wet.

"Hurry up," Mr. Stewart said.

I thought I'd better go to the bathroom too, while I had the chance. The man behind the counter pointed down a hall.

In the bathroom, Lily went first. "Do you think we're going to miss the game?" she asked from behind the stall door.

"No," I said, unsure. The bathroom stank of ammonia but didn't seem at all clean. Lily came out and went immediately to the sink to wash her hands. I was torn. I didn't want to use this bathroom but I didn't want to ask Mr. Stewart to stop later.

"Wait for me," I said to Lily, locking the door.

"I can't breathe," she said. "It stinks."

The bond between us seemed to be eroding in the face of so much filth and confusion. Had it occurred to me I would have told her that our only hope was to stick together. But she, clearly, wanted to return to the protection of her father. Some sort of filial loyalty apparently had blinded her to his weaknesses, his basic incompetence. It was obvious to me that he didn't have the faintest idea of how to take care of two young girls.

"Lily," I said, "if you don't wait for me—"

But she was already gone.

I sat on the toilet and stared at words scratched into the metal walls. They were words I knew I ought not to read, and so I didn't read them. The door creaked open and I said, "Lily?"

No one answered. I heard footsteps. I hadn't even finished going to the bathroom but I was already pulling up my pants. Then I saw a man's face peeking under the stall door and I couldn't move. I stared at his face, into his eyes, at his beard, not so that I would remember him but, precisely, so that I would forget.

He smiled and I came unfrozen and moved to the back of the stall. He withdrew and laughed and to my amazement, began humming. It sounded like "London Bridge." His voice softened as he moved back. I heard the door open and close. I flushed the toilet, opened the stall door and he was no longer in the bathroom.

There was no sign of him, either, in the hall. I hurried back into the coffee shop and there was Lily, sitting on a stool, waiting for the man behind the counter to finish blending a milk shake for her. She didn't look at me. Mr. Stewart was counting money. "No, no," he said, irritated. "The milk shakes are to go."

I accepted my own tall paper cup with straw and stood by the cash register, a few feet behind Mr. Stewart. Someone had put a small glass vase of fresh flowers into the shrine and rearranged the squat candles.

There was also, now, a framed picture of a young, dark-haired girl who, I suddenly believed, was either sick or dying. I could have said a quick prayer for this girl but I didn't and knew that this was wicked of me.

We left the coffee shop and it was still raining, though not as hard as before. Apparently, Mr. Stewart had gotten directions. He drove with more confidence and before long, we saw the high concrete walls of the Orange Bowl. This time, before I got out of the car, I put on my raincoat. The milk shake, however, had given me a chill and midway through the second quarter, I began to shiver and sneeze.

But I watched the game intently. So did Lily. During the first quarter, there was no score and both teams slipped and slid in the mud, and both quarterbacks got sacked. Mr. Stewart got up in disgust and took my twenty dollars and went to buy hot dogs. While he was gone, a Miami punt was blocked and Junior Davis, a lumbering defensive lineman for the Spartans, fell on the ball in the end zone. Lily and I screamed and cheered and jumped up and down in the puddles. After that, the game's momentum changed. Freddie Isaiah threw a touchdown pass. At half time the score was fourteen to three in favor of the Spartans and Lily and I were ecstatic.

At the beginning of the third quarter, Mr. Stewart mentioned leaving. Lily pleaded but Mr. Stewart shook his head and I knew then that he didn't care in the least about the Spartans and whether or not they won. Lily said she wanted to stay till the very end, and I said, "Yes, I do too." I couldn't believe that Mr. Stewart would bring us all this way and then suggest we leave with one quarter to go.

Miami scored a fluky touchdown when a Spartan defender slipped and fell and the Miami receiver was wide open for a pass. The stadium roared. That's when I began to feel sick, feverish, and in my head I could hear my mother scolding me for having gone out in the rain without my raincoat. "You're going to catch pneumonia," she was saying. I closed my eyes and said a prayer for the Spartans but I was afraid God wasn't listening to me anymore.

The men sitting behind us, who had been drinking beer all afternoon, began calling Freddie Isaiah bad names. They were drunk and they knew, from our heartfelt cheering, that we loved Freddie Isaiah. "That stupid nigger can't throw worth beans," one of them shouted right into my ear. I looked at Mr. Stewart, hoping he would come to Freddie's defense, but he didn't say anything.

In fact, I had heard Mr. Stewart use the word himself, once or twice, though not, specifically, in reference to Freddie Isaiah. I realized he was ashamed to be sitting with two girls who were rooting for a black man, and it didn't surprise me at all when he stood and said, "Okay, girls, get your things. I want to beat the traffic."

Lily whined and then couldn't hold back her tears. I tried to stall by pretending my knapsack wouldn't unzip, and then taking a long time to get out my umbrella. Somebody shouted "Down in front" and Mr. Stewart sat back down.

"Daddy, please," Lily said, "let us stay."

"Lily, damn it," Mr. Stewart roared. He grabbed her arm and shook her. "How many times do I have to tell you—"

"Daddy," Lily shrieked and Mr. Stewart hit her.

He smacked the side of the head and she cried out, reached up and held her ear. "Geez," one of the drunk men said.

"Now you stop that whining," Mr. Stewart said, "and do what I tell you." He turned and the way he ignored Lily made it seem as if he himself were shocked by what he'd done. Lily cried quietly, holding the side of her head.

I looked around, feeling embarrassed. Other people around us were staring disapprovingly. Mostly they were women. The men were watching the game.

"Lily, look," I whispered, nudging her.

Freddie Isaiah had taken the snap and was fading back, looking for a receiver. I could see Smithers open down the sideline. "Smithers," I shouted as loudly as I could. Lily stopped crying and looked towards Smithers. I stood and Lily stood and Freddie threw the ball. The men behind me went silent. I cheered, knowing, the minute the ball left Freddie's hand, that Smithers was going to catch it. And catch it he did, with hardly a stretch. The ball just dropped into his arms.

Without even watching him score the final touchdown, I turned to the men behind me. "There," I said. "You see?"

Then I looked at Mr. Stewart in the same way. I thought for a moment that he might haul off and hit me too. But he was not my father.

Lily was jumping up and down and throwing her arms up towards heaven. She seemed to have forgotten everything but the Spartans. They managed to hold on and win, despite the fact that we had to leave before the game was over. The victory, which we heard announced on the radio as we drove back to the airport, temporarily restored my faith in God. But it was a faith destined not to last. It wasn't long after that glorious Spartan season that I lost my faith not only in God but also in adults.

Lily, however, maintained her beliefs, and to this day, is a devout Catholic. When her father died, I went to the visitation though I hadn't seen the Stewarts in years. For some reason, I chose that moment to tell her about the man who had peeked under the bathroom stall. She said, "You're kidding?" and stood, giggling, beside her father's casket. Occasionally she looked down at the lid with a puzzled expression, as if she didn't believe her father was in there. At the funeral the next day, I watched her sit, tearless, beside her mother, and for a brief moment I found myself entertaining the notion of heaven—a heaven where Mr. Stewart would be welcome. It was a heaven which had no appeal for me, and I'm sorry to say it was the only sort of heaven I could imagine.

THE HAND IS QUICKER THAN THE HEART

Virginia rewound the tape and listened for the third time to the message Conrad had left. "Charlie and the Cheesepuffs are playing tonight. I'm going with a bunch of friends." He paused and added in a furtive tone, "Maybe you could meet me there."

Though the invitation wasn't very flattering—he hadn't dropped all his plans, lied to his wife and found a way to spend Friday night alone with her—she liked his sleepy voice, the fact that it was there, on tape.

She sat motionless in the rocking chair, sipping a cup of coffee. No breeze came through the jalousie windows. There had been no thunderstorm that afternoon.

She ran her finger across the oily skin of her thigh, leaving a distinct white trail—too much sun. She and Tracy, her old college roommate, had just returned from the beach.

"Look," Tracy said, raising her arm. The underside was splotched with a rash-like burn.

"That's going to peel," Virginia said.

Tracy produced a bottle of Vitamin E oil and a tin of Bayer aspirin. For someone from Boston, she was remarkably knowledgeable about after-tanning procedure.

"Are you tired?" Virginia asked. "Do you want to go tonight?"

"Do you think the band'll be good?"

"I've never heard them. That's not really the point."

Tracy picked the sand from between her toes. Even *they* were pink. "It's okay with me," she said, rising, heading for the shower.

Virginia put on a calypso record. She lay flat on the wooden floor, tapping her feet, the coffee cup teetering on her stomach. A roach crawled out from under the bookshelf, feeling its way towards the kitchen. She didn't bother to kill it. She was excited to see Conrad later that night. Even if his wife were there, Virginia might still find a moment to dance with him, get close enough to remind him of the afternoons at her house, when he brought champagne and ice cream or expensive chocolates and they sat on the floor and ate. "They always try and fatten you up," said one of her friends. "So no one else will want you."

"Where are my cigarettes?" Virginia asked herself out loud. She took a new pack from the carton in the kitchen, lit one and lay back down on the floor. The smoke hung near the ceiling in flat vaporous sheets. The bass line of the calypso thumped through the floor boards. She decided to think of all the men she'd kissed in the last several months: John, who was probably gay but wouldn't admit it; another John, who had been a detective in Manhattan for twenty years; Kevin's fiancée's brother in Atlanta during Spring break; and finally, last weekend, David, a friend from high school. They'd made out in the parking lot after drinking beer and playing pool at the Tiny Tap.

A lot of men. Still, she'd only kissed them. Conrad was the only one she'd slept with.

She walked to the sliding glass door and frowned at the honeysuckle clinging to the trellis. She had always hated the smell of honeysuckle, but what was the point of pulling it up? She tapped her foot, not in time to the music. Suddenly she needed to go out, eat, do something.

THE HAND IS QUICKER THAN THE HEART

"Leave me some hot water," she yelled to Tracy, though she always took a cold shower after a day at the beach. The sun had gone down. It was time to get going. She rested her cheek against the pane of the glass door and watched the shadows, like stains across the yard. Things were happening out there, with or without her. She didn't want to miss them.

✢ ✢ ✢

At Jimmie Mac's, where they stopped for dinner, there were no empty tables. They ordered hamburgers and french fries at the bar.

"Remember what we used to eat for dinner in Santa Cruz?" Tracy said. "We made everything with tofu."

Darrell Rogers walked through the door, pausing at the popcorn dispenser to fill a waxed paper bag. He poured a stream of popcorn into his mouth and munched, looking for someone he knew.

Virginia motioned him to an empty barstool. "What are you doing here, all by yourself?"

Darrell shrugged. "It's so hot." He fanned himself. "I had to get out of the house."

When their hamburgers came, Tracy and Virginia both gave him mounds of fries. "We really shouldn't." Tracy patted her stomach.

Darrell dismissed her with a wave of his hand and smiled his gap-toothed smile.

Virginia remembered that the last time she'd run into him, he'd mentioned getting together for lunch. She leaned her shoulder against his. The beer was going to her head, or maybe it was too much sun.

"It's nice to see you," she said.

Darrell wanted to go to the Cheesepuffs, too, and drove them to Ybor Square. In the car they smoked a joint and listened to a tape he'd brought back from Nigeria. He had been a disc jockey for the public radio station, but now he read the evening news.

Ybor Square was an old cigar factory, renovated and turned into a mall. The area had a bad reputation because of crack. Several people had been shot outside El Popo, the gay bar down the street.

The three of them walked through the courtyard under an orange-tinted sky. Virginia was alert, the marijuana heightening her senses. "I'm here," she said telepathically to Conrad, half-expecting him to pick that moment to walk into the plaza for a cigarette.

When she entered the nightclub, Conrad looked up. He sat at the head of a long table full of people, talking with the ease of a performer. Every winter he worked as a magician for a small circus that traveled around Florida.

Barb, his wife, smiled and held him by the arm, as if to keep him seated.

"The whole gang's here," Darrell shouted above the music. "Do you know Con and Barb? I used to work for them, at their furniture store."

Darrell walked straight to their table, which became a confusion of people standing, sitting, shaking hands, extending cheeks to be kissed. Virginia hung back with Tracy near the door. She hadn't known that Conrad and Barb owned a furniture store.

"Which one is he?" Tracy asked.

"The one looking over here."

"They're all looking over here."

THE HAND IS QUICKER THAN THE HEART

Virginia had never met any of the people staring at them. "Shit," she said softly. "Let's get this over with."

She didn't listen to names. She let her eyes rest briefly, politely, on Conrad, then calculated the right sort of smile—a Friday night, decadent smile. He looked back with such obvious pleasure that her eyes widened in excitement and alarm.

Barb, whom she'd met once before at a party, smiled at her, too. She had cut off all her hair, which made her look older but more handsome. She kept her hand on Conrad's arm, rubbing it as if to calm him. Her other hand was wrapped around the stem of a cocktail glass containing a pink mixture topped with a parasol.

Darrell continued his introductions. A dark-haired woman at the end of the table stared at Virginia with malevolence. The look was so mean that Virginia stepped back and the smile dropped from her face. She felt an involuntary rush of shame in her stomach, as if she'd been caught doing something wrong.

"Sit down," Conrad said, nodding towards the chair next to his. Virginia gave him a helpless look as Darrell pulled her onto the dance floor.

"Two of them," said a man at the table. "How did Darrell manage that?"

"Shake it up, baby," sang Charlie, who during the day was a reporter for Channel 12. He smiled down at the dancers. The Cheesepuffs were the two back-up singers, both twisting and shouting.

Conrad brought a tall woman in a miniskirt onto the dance floor. He seemed happy, smiling at everyone—Virginia, his dancing partner, and the people at his table across the room. When the song ended, he kissed the woman on the lips, then disappeared alone down a hall.

Virginia led Darrell and Tracy to a small table away from the dance floor. She didn't want to sit with Conrad's group.

"Chin chin," said Darrell, raising his bottle.

"Who are all those people?" Virginia asked.

"The guys are film makers from Miami. The women live here. They're artists." He leaned close to Virginia. "Rachel—" he whispered.

"Which one's she?"

"Dark hair."

"Yeah, what about her? She's awful."

"Rachel," Darrell began slowly, lifting his eyebrows, building suspense. "Rachel is having a torrid affair with Con."

Virginia took a gulp of beer. She lit a cigarette. Her fingers shook and she looked down at her hand, holding the match, the flame shrinking and blackening the wood till it curled.

She looked at Darrell. "How do you know?"

"She told me. We're friends."

Virginia turned to Rachel, who sat immobile, not smiling or talking to anyone. Rachel gathered her dark hair up in one hand and rolled her wine glass across her cheek, cooling herself with the tiny drops of condensation.

Virginia looked down the hall where Conrad had disappeared. What if he'd invited Rachel, too? Left the same message on her machine, suggested in his sexy voice that she meet him here? It was one thing to be married, then take on a lover. But how many affairs was Conrad having?

THE HAND IS QUICKER THAN THE HEART

"I wouldn't want to get on her bad side," Darrell said.

Rachel's eyes narrowed as if she knew they were talking about her. Then she laughed, unprompted. The sound came from deep in her chest, like a cough.

"What exactly does torrid mean?" Virginia wondered out loud.

"You know what it means." Darrell frowned and drummed his fingertips on the table. Tracy leaned forward, curious.

Virginia said, "It's not a word I often hear."

"Think of everything a great affair is supposed to be," Darrell said with a sigh. "Illicit. Passionate. Completely out of control."

The words produced an instant picture in Virginia's mind, of Conrad and Rachel in each other's arms. She couldn't stop the image, which began to move, like a porno film, horrifying, magnified.

Tracy piped in, "Who's having this great affair?"

"Shhh," Darrell said. "Rachel and Con."

Tracy's face revealed all the shock Virginia was trying to hide. Virginia shook her head and pressed her lips, in a gesture that said, Don't give me away. Later, when the night was over, she and Tracy would talk.

"And you?" Virginia turned quickly to Darrell. "Are you having any torrid affairs?" She was trying to be flirtatious, but there was something desperate in her voice. The question sounded accusatory.

Darrell looked at her with surprise. "My wife asked me the same thing tonight."

"Your wife?" Virginia said. "I didn't know you were married."

He took off his glasses and pressed the two spots they left on his nose. "I may not be for much longer."

"Chin chin." Tracy raised her glass in a melancholy gesture, with an expression on her face that seemed to say, this is why people come to bars and drink.

One of the Miami film makers appeared at the table. "Hey, Kirk," Darrell said, pumping Kirk's hand so thoroughly that his whole body shook.

"We're going for a swim at Rachel's," Kirk said, extracting himself, "if you want to come."

Conrad appeared behind him. "Come," he said to Virginia. "Everybody wants you to come."

"Everybody?" she asked, one eyebrow raised.

He slid his finger down her neck. His eyes were red around the rims—she remembered from their naps how his eyes never completely closed during sleep. One black curl had fallen across his forehead. She was amazed he didn't detect her anger.

She knew she ought to ask Darrell to drive them home. She and Tracy ought to finish the night by lying in bed and laughing at a horror movie or the late show. But she wanted to discover Rachel's house, to secretly invade her territory.

"We'll see," she said to Conrad. She touched Darrell's elbow and said, "Dance with me." The second set had already begun. She and Darrell danced until they were sweaty and the others had left. Tracy nursed her beer alone at the table, stretching and yawning, ready to go.

☩ ☩ ☩

Conrad leaned back against the kitchen counter, next to an enormous pile of dirty dishes. He stretched a short piece of white rope

THE HAND IS QUICKER THAN
THE HEART

between his hands and asked Virginia, who stood beside him, to cut it in half with the butcher knife.

Darrell looked up from the joint he was rolling at the table. Tracy stood by the refrigerator. The others, including Rachel, had stopped talking and moved into the light at the top step where the sliding glass doors opened onto the patio.

Barb had never made it to Rachel's. Virginia didn't know how Conrad had gotten rid of her.

Virginia aimed the knife at Conrad and with the tip of the blade, pricked the fibers of his shirt. Then she sawed at the rope, with a downward motion. It wasn't easy to cut.

"What a good assistant," Conrad said when the rope finally snapped. He tied the two pieces together and pulled it tight, all in one piece again. He put the rope back into a drawer filled with extension cords, bottles of glue and scissors.

"Was that a real rope?" Virginia asked, looking into the drawer.

"Sure."

"Not a trick rope?"

"No. The trick was here." He showed his empty palms. Virginia half expected him to reach up, behind her ear, and bring out a quarter. She smiled, turned and gazed out the window. Down the block two waiters, still in uniform, emerged from a bar and hurried down the street, as if to an assignation.

At the first opportunity, Virginia had asked Conrad about Rachel. "It was over a long time ago," had been his immediate answer. He'd wanted to know who'd started the rumor, but she had lied, protected Darrell, said no one had told her anything.

It was hard for her to know whom to believe. The decision would have to be arbitrary. If she believed Conrad, she could continue with him. She wasn't prepared to do otherwise. She turned to him and said, "Can I be your assistant again some time?" and gave him a sleepy look.

He reacted with instant attention. He didn't move but somehow she felt he'd gotten closer.

She saw Rachel out of the corner of her eye, standing on the threshold of the sliding glass doors, neither in nor out of the house. She wore a green army shirt with stripes of rank on the shoulders. Her jeans were tight all the way down her legs and on her feet were a pair of black, high-heeled sandals.

Virginia turned to Tracy. "Are you tired?"

Tracy shook her head. "Weird night."

Everyone seemed to be in a trance. Conrad unscrewed the top of a bottle of tequila, and with a flick of his wrist, took a swig. His Adam's apple went up and down while air bubbled back into the bottle. He set it down and looked at his watch. "Do you realize how late it is? What are we doing here?"

She looked at his wrist. It was four in the morning. No one was thinking of leaving. Darrell lit the joint and passed it to Frank, the other man from Miami.

"How about a swim?" Frank suggested to no one in particular. He exhaled a huge amount of smoke.

"He's a sleaze bag," Tracy whispered, looking at Frank. "He came up and stuck his hand between my legs."

THE HAND IS QUICKER THAN THE HEART

Rachel moved slowly through the kitchen. She was dark and solid, everything Virginia was not. Her hips rolled as she walked. Conrad stared after her.

"It *is* true," Virginia said to him quietly.

"No," he pleaded. "I promise you."

Someone put on a Burning Spear album. Kirk approached and took Virginia's hand. They assumed a waltzing position. "Are you going to go swimming?" Kirk asked.

"Maybe," she said and cast a smile over her shoulder at Conrad.

"Where did you come from?" Kirk leaned down to speak, dancing her into the hall. "I've never heard of you before."

She looked up at his face, not sure what he meant. She tried to follow his steps, but evidently he was dancing not to the reggae, but to some other tune he was hearing.

"From Tampa," she answered.

"No, I mean whose friend are you?"

"Conrad's."

He sighed and pulled her close. "Con has a lot of friends."

"What do you mean?"

He didn't answer. He waltzed her into the dining room and they circled a large table covered with piles of mail, magazines and newspapers. She wanted to find out what he meant but she didn't ask again. She had no idea who he was, why he was in Tampa, how he knew Conrad. No one made any references to the past.

Darrell shuffled and swayed in the living room, his eyes closed, dancing by himself. The smell of the marijuana reached them from the kitchen.

It was ridiculous to be waltzing to reggae, but Kirk held her more and more tightly.

Rachel carried a bundle of towels through the dining room, carefully avoiding eye contact with anyone. She headed for the swimming pool in the backyard, which was exotically beautiful, like a German spa. There were statues around the edge of the pool and fountains shaped like cupids.

"It's one of those hot August nights." Kirk let his arm slip down to her waist. "It's so hot we need to swim."

Virginia smelled his skin through his shirt—no soap, no cologne, just plain fresh skin. He was a handsome man, well-built, good features. His eyes were constantly narrowing in the contemplation of some sensual pleasure.

She was getting her second wind, a reckless feeling, a desire to stay up the rest of the night. Then she and Tracy could walk back along the Bayshore in their night-time clothes and leer at the Saturday joggers.

The song ended and Kirk kissed her. His mouth was lazy and dry. Darrell watched from the living room. "A swim?" Darrell called out when Kirk let her go. "A drunken skinny-dip?"

"The water's cold," Virginia said.

"It'll wake us up."

She took Darrell's arm. "Are you feeling all right?" she asked as they walked to the kitchen. Kirk traipsed behind.

"Better, better," Darrell assured her.

"You don't think your wife's worrying about you?"

THE HAND IS QUICKER THAN THE HEART

Darrell shook his head. "I'm sure she's been out all night, too. I'll probably beat her home."

"You're not leaving?" She tightened her grip.

"No." He shook his head. He brought his face close to hers, squinting through his round wire-rimmed glasses. She thought he was going to say, "This is how the Eskimos kiss," and rub her nose with his.

Instead he turned and asked Kirk about his latest film. The two of them continued out to the pool. Virginia stopped in the kitchen, where Conrad was talking to Rachel's roommate Melissa, who couldn't seem to stand still. She had on a black and white print dress with a wide, billowy skirt, and a pair of ancient platform shoes. Virginia leaned against the refrigerator, not too close to Conrad.

"You met Darrell in Nicaragua," Melissa said.

Conrad looked up. "You did?"

"We were staying at the same pension in Managua," Virginia said.

"What were you doing there?" Conrad asked.

"Learning Spanish."

"That's very special," Melissa said. "Meeting Darrell like that."

Virginia smiled. Yes, she supposed it was special—to meet somebody in Managua and then run into them again several years later. The funny thing was that she and Darrell hadn't spent much time together in Central America. They hadn't seemed to like each other.

Melissa twirled in the center of the room. The lace frill of a petticoat stuck out from beneath her skirt. "You and Darrell will always be friends," she said prophetically, and, as if to emphasize the drama of her words, she walked immediately out the door.

Instantly Virginia was aware of being alone with Conrad. She flattened the small of her back against the refrigerator. Conrad walked closer, until he was within touching distance. He faced her but she looked straight ahead, out the blackened window.

The overhead light blinded her to the outside. But the people by the pool, whoever they were, had a clear view of the kitchen.

"Kirk asked about you," Conrad said. "He's completely taken."

Her breathing became faster. She didn't care about Kirk. She almost said so, but waited instead for what Conrad would say next. Their aloneness seemed dangerous. It wasn't going to last.

Conrad moved closer. "I can see your breath," he said. She thought about the way you could see particles of dust in a beam of light.

"Breathe on me," he whispered.

His request startled her and she almost laughed. She turned her head and tried to let out some of her breath. Her chest was tight. "Do it," he said. "It's the closest I can get to you."

She forgot about the others seeing through the sliding glass doors. She blew out and at the same time Conrad breathed in. When he exhaled she smelled cigarette smoke and tequila. Things flashed in her mind, like they were supposed to before you died. She remembered that once he'd told her she was beautiful, in a believable way. "When I first saw you," he'd said, "I didn't notice you. Then I *saw* you. And I thought, My God, she's beautiful. How did I ever not notice?"

Once she'd been walking down Bayshore near his house, that fast kind of walking that made her dizzy and able to see and understand things. She'd thought, what if he becomes my greatest love? What if she

THE HAND IS QUICKER THAN THE HEART

gave up, surrendered, not her pride or self-interest, but her center, the magnet inside her that held everything together, that kept her from spilling into a pile of flesh. What if he could make that happen? Could he?

"Deeper," he said. "Breathe deeper."

She pushed her breath out again and turned, leaning into the refrigerator. She knew she couldn't touch Conrad, because of all the people. He couldn't touch her either. She hugged herself around the middle as if she felt sick, but instead of doubling over, she lifted her chin, stretched her neck and despite everything, wished he would kiss her, no matter who saw.

"Let's go," she said. "Walk home with me."

"I wish I could." He looked nervously towards the pool. "I'm not used to being with you in public. I'm not used to stopping myself."

"Let's go," she said. "Just outside."

He left first and she waited. She found a tumbler and poured a sip of tequila. She took her time, stretched everything out. Who did she think they were fooling?

Outside, he was sitting on the bumper of someone's truck, looking in the direction of his house. She hadn't realized until that moment that he and Rachel lived on the same street.

Conrad stood when she approached but kept an eye on his house. Though she had only spent afternoons with him, she was accustomed to his undivided attention. She touched his arm. He turned abruptly and stepped mechanically towards her.

"Are you okay?" she asked, as he held her.

"What a strange night," he said.

A rat ran across the telephone wire above them. It stopped and balanced, its tail flicking angrily. Then it was off again, disappearing down the other side of a pole. Conrad didn't look up. Was he nervous about Barb? Did he think she might come walking back down the street?

"Conrad," she said. He held her chin and kissed her, as if to keep her from talking. "Con, tell me what's going on."

"It's very complicated," he said in a soft, distracted voice.

She felt herself begin to panic. What could be complicated? He'd denied the affair with Rachel. Was there something else? In her experience, when a man said things were complicated, it was a sign of trouble, a sign that the end was near.

She immediately began to search for something—a gesture, a sentence—that would pull all his actions together, explain him, tell her what to expect.

"I haven't been honest with you," he said.

She felt wild and illogical. She remembered that once, quickly, he'd told her that he loved her. He'd never repeated it. He must have been lying.

He hung his head, scuffed his toe on the asphalt. He wasn't going to volunteer anything. She would have to guess and probe, coax his confession out of him like a lawyer.

"About what?" she asked, nearly out of breath.

"I don't know. My life's out of control."

"What do you mean, out of control?"

THE HAND IS QUICKER THAN THE HEART

He walked away and peered down the street. She sat on the bumper of the truck. It was cold through her jeans and she felt the pattern in the metal. "Damn it," she said to herself.

"I'm sorry," Conrad said, his back to her.

"Just tell me." Her voice was whining.

"I can't."

"What do you mean, you can't? Why can't you?"

He turned and walked back to the truck and misjudged the distance between himself and the bumper, sitting so heavily that the rear end bounced and creaked. She realized how drunk he was. For some reason, that calmed her.

"I'd rather know the truth," she said. "Really. I don't care what it is. For me, it's better to know." She was lying, but more than fear, she felt curiosity, like wanting to watch the gory parts of a movie, when most people close their eyes.

Conrad said, "I don't think I've ever told the truth to anyone."

Was this the bait? Was this how he would set her apart, make her feel special? No, he was simply asking her to play a role—the mistress, the confidante, the understanding one.

"I've told bits and pieces," he said, "but never the whole truth."

They both heard footsteps and looked towards the door. It was Frank. He looked around the front yard, turned, and walked back into the house.

"We're missed," Conrad said.

"I wish we could leave."

"Me, too." He put his hand behind her neck and pulled her towards him. She leaned against him at an awkward angle. When he kissed her, their front teeth knocked.

More footsteps. This time it was Rachel, standing in the light of the porch, looking directly at them. She marched down the steps and into the street. She walked right up to them. There was no time to say anything, no time to escape.

"I want to talk to you," she said to Conrad, forcing Virginia to step back.

"Well," Virginia said.

Conrad lifted his hand to wave goodbye. Virginia looked at them once before turning. She walked back to the porch and sat on the steps. Frank was there, as if he were waiting for something. It seemed like all night everyone had been waiting.

"Tracy was looking for you," he said.

Virginia stared at him.

"I'm sorry," he said. "Rachel wanted me to find Con. I didn't want to come out here."

"What the hell is going on?" Virginia said. Frank looked like a Miami gangster in his black shirt.

Rachel appeared at the edge of the front walk. She sat on the steps, opposite Virginia. Her face revealed nothing. For a while, no one spoke.

Virginia knew she ought to go home. But something told her to stay, that it would be interesting to stay, that eventually someone would have to say something. If she sat on the steps next to Rachel long enough, Rachel would have to say *something*.

THE HAND IS QUICKER THAN THE HEART

"Where did Con go?" Frank asked.

"How should I know?" Rachel snapped.

"He didn't say where he was going?"

"I don't think it's any of your business," she said and rose to go into the house.

"She's a bitch," Frank said.

"I need to go home." Virginia leaned back against the stairs and looked down the street. At that moment, Conrad was probably unlocking his front door, walking up the stairs and quietly entering his study. Barb was asleep. She would never know anything. Even if she guessed, Conrad would deny it. It occurred to Virginia that however crazy or complicated they seemed, these people were not acting out of passion. Not even Rachel, who seemed so angry and jealous. They were bored. They had bad habits.

"No one went swimming," Frank said. "Nothing happened."

"What did you expect?" Virginia asked.

He shrugged. "An orgy?"

She gave him a disgusted look.

"You're a lovely girl." He laughed and touched her cheek.

She turned away. "Sometimes," she said, not exactly to Frank. "I just want someone to explain things."

Frank leaned forward and parted his lips. His tongue lay flat against the bottom of his mouth, as if he were about to start panting. "I just want to get laid," he said.

She stood and yelled Darrell's name twice.

"Hey," Frank said. "The neighbors."

She wanted to tell Frank how repulsive he was. She wanted to be a bitch, like Rachel. She realized that inside her there *was* a Rachel, a woman who wore tough clothes and high heels, who was savvy and stayed up all night and tricked herself into thinking it was living, really living.

Darrell and Tracy walked out the front door. Both of them had wet hair. Tracy was carrying her shoes.

"Did you know there's a whirlpool back there?" Darrell asked.

"What did I miss?" Frank moaned.

"It's bed time," Tracy said, pointing to the light in the eastern sky. She turned to Darrell. "See what I mean?"

"Yes," he answered, offering her his arm.

The understanding they'd come to—whatever it was—irritated Virginia. It might have been perfectly friendly, benign. But she didn't want to be near them.

No one bothered going back in the house. No one spoke to Frank. He sat motionless on the stairs, looking up, desperately wanting to be included, to be invited if only as far as Virginia's couch, where surely he would have given up, like the rest of them, and finally gone to sleep.

HURRY HOME

One morning my father announced that he was volunteering for the army. The whole family was at the breakfast table, none of us quite awake—me, my stepmother Bonnie, and Raymond and Kitty, my father's youngest children.

Bonnie sprinkled a teaspoon of sugar over her Special K. In the silence that followed my father's announcement, the sugar made a strange sifting noise as it fell through the flakes to the bottom of the bowl.

"You have to understand," Dad said. "I've been—" He hesitated. "—called."

He didn't mean drafted; he meant he'd found a new vocation. He poured milk from a glass pitcher over his cereal and calmly took a bite. From his mouth came a cracking sound: his jaw popping as he chewed.

"Your mother and I have discussed this," he continued, gazing down his nose at Raymond and Kitty. He had a stern look on his face, as if he might be about to punish them. Then he glanced over at me and he looked embarrassed, and I was sure, for a moment, he'd forgotten I was there.

I had moved in with my father a month ago, in order to get to know him. He had left home, the house in Atlanta where my mother still lived, when I was six. Now I was almost fifteen. It wasn't that there was something wrong with my mother. I hadn't left *her*. But my father was like a character out of a book, an adventurer or a hero, and I had wanted to be near him.

My mother had been against the idea but hadn't tried to stop me. She had consulted Bonnie, Dad's third wife. It was Bonnie, not my father, who had made it possible for me to live there—by inviting me and also by reassuring my mother. Bonnie was small and thin with dark hair that flipped at her shoulders, entirely different from my mother, who was blonde and sharp-featured and aristocratic. My father's first wife, whom I'd only seen pictures of, was the most unusual of all his wives—a muscular woman with a square jaw, the daughter of a rancher in Nevada. She had the first two children, both boys, who rode horses and led the lives of cowboys.

In between bites, with his mouth full, Dad said, "I want to go to Vietnam."

Bonnie flinched. For a moment she stopped eating. I noticed for the first time how swollen her eyes were. She had obviously spent the night crying and arguing with him.

I didn't know much about Vietnam—only that it was far away. I rarely watched the news. Once I'd listened to a dinner conversation among my mother and her friends, all of whom were against the war.

"I'll be an officer," Dad continued. "Anyone with a degree is automatically an officer."

My father had had lots of jobs, lots of "callings," nearly all of them involving the use of his hands. He'd been a minor league catcher, a trumpeter in a jazz band and now he taught at the deaf institute. His younger brother, my uncle, had been deaf all his life and that's how my father had learned sign language. Even when my father spoke to people who could hear, his hands sometimes traced the outlines of words.

None of us said anything. The smell of the paper mill drifted in through the open windows. It was April and unseasonably warm. The daffodils in the yard, which had opened upon my arrival, were shriveling, turning crackly brown. Beyond the flower beds, in the distance, were the Blue Ridge Mountains. Each morning when I woke up and looked out, I thought about climbing those mountains, trudging up till I reached the top. They were the most beautiful mountains I'd ever seen, not that I'd seen many. I had spent my whole life in a city. North Carolina was different from Atlanta, different from Georgia: the bricks of the houses were a softer red, the roads narrower, and the smells, not just unusual smells like the paper mill—even rain and grass smelled different. The school was ten times smaller than the one I'd gone to, and the teachers taught different subjects to the ninth grade. But I had caught up quickly. In fact, later that day I had a geography quiz and even though I hadn't quite finished my homework—shaded the blank maps using Kitty's colored pencils—I wasn't worried about making an A.

My father leaned back, having finished his cereal. "When I was young," he began, "I thought I would join the Air Force. One summer Mother and Father rented a house in Florida. I spent a lot of time with the next door neighbor, Lieutenant Murphy. He had just come back from the war. He was an Air Force pilot. He'd been shot down over the Pacific."

My father leaned forward and gripped the table. I didn't know who he was talking to. Bonnie was watching him as if she might, at any moment, burst into tears. The kids were fidgety. Kitty dipped her spoon over and over into the sugary leftover milk in her bowl while Raymond played with his napkin, tearing it into jagged strips which he then carefully rolled into small paper torpedoes. When Bonnie softly touched his hand, he stopped.

All I could think of was that I had just arrived and already my father was leaving. Not just leaving, but going to war. Of course I didn't believe he would die. He was much too clever for that.

But as we lingered over breakfast, I wondered if his sudden decision had something to do with me. I swallowed and felt a lump in my throat. My arrival had upset the balance, even though I hadn't asked for anything special—no privileges or attention. I'd slept in the other twin bed in Kitty's room and eaten like a bird. Even Bonnie had encouraged me to eat more.

I wanted to say, Wait! Let *me* leave. Then everything would be normal again. I was old enough to know that my father wasn't just my father. He was Bonnie's husband, and Raymond and Kitty, who were four and six, needed him much more than I did.

I thought of running away, slipping off in the middle of the night and walking to the Greyhound station, leaving a sad, grateful note they would find in the morning.

But I knew, somehow, it wouldn't do any good. Dad had already made up his mind. He was gazing out the window of the house as if it was the window of a transport plane and below him was a jungle full of soldiers and tanks.

"Lieutenant Murphy was the bravest man I ever knew," he continued. "He used to take me deep sea fishing. He told me his son was a no-good drunk. He sort of adopted me. One afternoon we went out on his boat and a squall came up, out of nowhere. The waves were huge, but then there was one really huge wave that hit the boat and just like that, she sank. We stayed with her and then the Coast Guard came.

Lieutenant Murphy gave me his St. Christopher's medal. He said it was the second time it had saved his life."

"Where is it now?" I asked, though I had already guessed.

Dad unbuttoned the middle two buttons of his shirt. The medal was the size of a silver dollar, tarnished and engraved. It was large enough to protect his heart from bullets.

He rose and put on his suit jacket. The edges of the sleeves and lapel were frayed, the white threads visible in places. He buttoned the top button of his shirt and tightened his tie.

Bonnie and I cleared the table. Raymond and Kitty, after being told several times, went upstairs and brushed their teeth. Dad dropped us at our separate schools—Raymond at nursery school, Kitty at elementary and finally me at junior high. In the moments when we were alone, Dad didn't say anything more about joining the army, nor did he make the special apology I'd hoped for. But before I opened the door to get out, he leaned over and kissed my cheek.

✢ ✢ ✢

During the two weeks before my father left, all I did was read. Bonnie took me to the public library and didn't object when I checked out three James Michener novels. She didn't say, "Those are adult books," or "You can't read four thousand pages in three weeks." *Hawaii*, my favorite, which I'd read before, was the one I saved for last.

Kitty's room, where I would go after school to lie down and read, was a mess of Barbies, troll dolls and plastic horses. Kitty had a small record player and a collection of yellow forty-fives. At night she insisted, and I didn't mind, that we listen to a recording of Dr. Seuss' "Sleep

Book." Before it was over, she'd be asleep. I would pick up the needle, trying not to make another scratch—the record was already covered with them—and read my novel by the weak amber beam of my flashlight until one or two in the morning.

I felt safe in the house, though it was close to a ravine thick with kudzu and poison ivy. The neighborhood kids said the ravine was full of escapees from the insane asylum. I had already been invited to the ravine by a boy at school, Aaron Chandler, but I was afraid of poison ivy, having once had a severe reaction, even bumps down the inside of my throat. I was afraid of Aaron Chandler, too—he was Jewish with long frizzy hair and fat around the middle. He bore an uncanny resemblance to Joe Cocker, the singer. Not only that, he had perfected an imitation—jerks and flails that ended with a hoarse piercing scream.

"Have you ever smoked grass?" he had wanted to know.

I shook my head.

"Come to the ravine and I'll give you a joint. You don't have to smoke it with me. You can take it home if you want."

To demonstrate good faith, he opened his pack of cigarettes and showed me the joint—yellow paper with twigs of marijuana sticking out. His fingers, though stained, were long and delicate, with perfectly rounded nails.

"Why don't you just give it to me now?" I asked.

He shook his finger, as if he were scolding. An unpleasant grin spread across his face. It was like a nightmare—I wanted to run, but his nearness, his unblinking eyes, the smell of cigarettes on his breath, held me as tightly as if he'd gripped my arms.

The next day he called me at the house. Bonnie said, "We're in the middle of dinner. May I ask who's calling?" I knew, in that horrible, stomach-sinking moment—it couldn't have been anyone but Aaron.

"Who's Aaron?" Bonnie asked, returning to the table. I tried to answer, but no sound came out. Bonnie smiled at my father, who raised an eyebrow. I nearly gagged on a mouthful of squash. I wanted to say, "I don't know anyone named Aaron. It must have been a wrong number. He must have been looking for another girl named Faye."

I lay in bed and imagined him lurking outside in the ravine. What if, all of a sudden, he threw stones at my window? Outside, Bonnie's dogs would bark and froth at the mouth, hurling themselves against the chain link fence. Everybody in the house would wake up. Oh, the thought of them seeing Aaron! There he would be, frozen on the front lawn. My father would grab him by the collar, look him up and down. Aaron would let out a wail and jerk like Joe Cocker. I would have to say, "It's Aaron. I don't know what he's doing here. Really I don't." My father, Bonnie, even little Raymond, would think I had been on my way out to meet him. They would think I was *interested* in a hideous boy like him.

I turned off my flashlight and folded the upper corner of the page I'd been reading. If Aaron was out there, he was content to watch from afar. The bed I was sleeping in was less comfortable than my bed at home, but it was pushed up against the wide double window and if I turned on my side, I could look directly out. I felt like I was sleeping in a room made of glass. Beyond the ravine was a thicket, and beyond that the lake, a flat black surface that reflected the mountains around us. A half moon came out from behind a cloud and made a wavy yellow line across the water.

I closed my eyes and just as I was about to fall asleep, I heard a strange sound. At first I thought it was part of a dream but I opened my eyes and strained my ears and soon I heard it again. Maybe someone was lying in the ravine, wounded. Instinctively I turned and checked on Kitty. She was still in bed asleep.

I propped myself up on one elbow and peered out the window. What if a murderer or lunatic had been watching me read? I dropped onto my stomach and tried to make myself flat, as if I were part of the sheets and blankets. The crying continued, faintly, somewhere off in the distance, then rose sharply in pitch—a sound that was soft but at the same time shrill, a cry that didn't sound human at all. One by one, the dogs began howling, at first tentatively, as if they didn't want to disturb anyone, then with full force. They sounded like wolves.

I looked everywhere, trying to find where the cry was coming from. I studied the thicket and the dark slash of the ravine. Then something glinted near the bank of the lake. I rubbed the fuzziness out of my eyes and looked again.

It was my father dressed in his robe and pajamas, standing at the edge of the trees, playing his trumpet.

He leaned back and a moment later, I heard a series of faint high notes. I couldn't make out the song he was playing. It could have been one of the songs he played at night after dinner, "Blue Moon" or "Someone Like You." He reared back, bent at the knees. The trumpet was aimed at the sky.

I watched him, my father, whom I'd seen only four times since I was six. He'd written me three letters, which I had saved and occasionally taken out to read. They were each about a page long, handwritten, every word composed of capital letters. Each told a story—of a deaf student who had been lonely until one day he began to sign; of Bonnie's prize Weimaraner, Fox, who had gotten his leg caught in a trap. For the most part, the letters could have been written by anyone, except that sometimes he mentioned Raymond and Kitty and sometimes he told me to say hello to my mother. Though he never said he loved me, I knew, from those letters, that he did.

I sat up in bed, the only witness, I thought, to my father's performance. Then a door slammed and a woman in a long white dress, her hair dark and loose, appeared at the far edge of the back lawn. She ran alongside the thicket above the ravine, then disappeared down the path to the lake.

My nose touched the glass, my breath making a small bloom of fog on the pane. The woman emerged from the trees and stood at the edge of the lake. Her back was to me, her face hidden, but it couldn't have been anyone but Bonnie. Dad watched her then started playing again. He swung his shoulders and moved the trumpet right and left. His song was upbeat and cheerful.

I thought Bonnie had run out of the house angry or upset. I had expected her to approach my father carefully, holding out her hand, asking for the trumpet as if it were a gun, talking softly to Dad as if to disarm him. But she stood, listening to the trumpet with one hand at her ear, then she twirled and her white robe flew out in all directions. The trumpet let out a loud, silly peal of laughter.

I laughed myself, watching Bonnie dance. She was an imp, a fairy, tilting her head and kicking her feet, and I wouldn't have been surprised had she and my father suddenly hopped onto the lily pads and skipped across the lake.

But as she closed in on my father, her dance came to a halt. He lowered the trumpet then dropped it. For a long time he stared at her. Then he put his hands under her robe and pushed it off. It fell in slow motion—past her shoulders, her back, her waist, until finally it lay in a white puddle around her feet.

She was naked and tiny, hardly big enough to be his wife. Her hair, not done in its usual flip, hung way past her shoulders. She stood there, waiting, and then my father leaned down and kissed her.

He dropped to his knees and pulled her with him. Their bodies disappeared, the dark green velour of his bathrobe covering them completely, making them blend into the grass. I stared for a long time. Once I caught a glimpse of Bonnie's knee, popping out from under the robe. Then I heard the trumpet playing again but it must have been my imagination. I could see it clearly, several feet away from them, lying neglected in the grass.

✢ ✢ ✢

My mother wrote me once a week and usually I answered right away. But I let ten days go by before I attempted to put into words how my father had enlisted in the army. My first letter contained an outright lie—I said that he'd been drafted. But I tore that up and tried again, this time coming closer to the truth: "Even though I won't be able to spend more time with him, what he's done makes me proud."

My mother would no doubt see through my sugary words and know that I was upset. She would be mad at my father. I could hear her say, "Your father doesn't think of anybody but himself."

But my father had the power to make people love him. Even my mother, no matter what she said, deep down still loved my father. If he ever went to her house and begged to be forgiven, she would take him back. Maybe not right away. For a few days she'd yell, scowl and stomp around the house, but gradually she'd soften. She'd sit in the living room while he practiced trumpet and slightly tap her foot. She'd remember how much he liked coconut cake; she'd let him kiss the back of her neck. That was the way I remembered them—dancing in the living room, martinis sloshing out of long-stemmed glasses (I always got one gin-soaked olive), playing long serious games of Spite and Malice on the screened porch, drinking beer under the light where dozens of gnats swarmed.

Still, I didn't tell her how I felt about my father leaving. She would insist that I return to Atlanta immediately, but I intended on staying. It was unreasonable, I was prepared to argue, for me to change schools twice in the middle of one year.

Why I wanted to remain at my father's house, even after he'd left, was something I couldn't explain. It had to do with Bonnie. I had always liked her, but after the night when I'd seen her by the lake, I felt more drawn to her than ever. She was the one I talked to, shopped with, helped in the kitchen. Remarkably, she didn't seem upset that Dad was leaving. Her eyes hadn't been swollen from crying except for that one morning. Of course, I didn't tell her what I'd seen out by the lake. But once in a while when she looked at me, my face would get hot, and I would think that somehow she had guessed.

I would also become embarrassed when my father played the trumpet. I couldn't watch him putting it to his lips. It was worse—

unbearable—when Bonnie leaned against the kitchen door, dried her hands on a dish towel, and listened, with a romantic expression on her face, to "Blue Moon."

My mother called the afternoon she got my letter. I had answered the phone in the kitchen and wanted to change to an upstairs phone. But my father, a few feet away in the den, seemed to be paying no attention to my side of the conversation. He was reading the newspaper.

My mother said it was fine for me to stay till school let out. Later, she said, we'd go on vacation.

There was a pause in the conversation and then she asked, "Why does your father want to go to Vietnam?"

"I don't know."

"He used to talk about joining the Air Force."

Outside, Bonnie was stepping through the daffodil beds, bending and pulling weeds. Her hands looked like balloons in her big gardening gloves.

"Do you want to talk to him?" I asked.

There was silence on the other end of the line.

"Damn," my father said softly, reading the baseball scores.

"Do you?" I asked again and suddenly I missed my mother terribly. She was just home from work, her jacket thrown across the back of the couch, her scarf unknotted, the tails hanging down like a man's loosened tie. A glass of iced tea, sweating, on a coaster on the counter. Her earrings removed so she could rub her pinched earlobes. Some hairs would have escaped from the back of her bun. I wanted to touch them, tickle her neck so that her head hung forward, her eyes closed, and she said, "Mm," and forgot about her hard day at the office.

"Sweetheart," she said. "Your father and I—"

If only I could tell her what he looked like now, relaxing in his recliner, his legs stretched out, his feet bare. His face was half-hidden by the top of the paper, which intensified the look of concentration in his eyes. He hadn't changed—his hair black, no gray, his build stocky, solid, like a catcher's ought to be. He had already passed his physical. The day he came home with the news—a thin report he carried, folded, in his back pocket—we had all been waiting, knowing it was the only real obstacle to his going. Bonnie had glanced over the report and I had expected her to be upset. But she slowly looked up from the paper to my father's eager face, and she gave him a smile, as if they had exchanged a funny secret. The kids shouted and leaped, repeating what my father had been telling them for days. "Daddy's going to be a soldier!" They shaped their hands like pistols. "Pow, pow!"

"Mom," I said, and my father looked up. Maybe he hadn't realized who I'd been talking to, or maybe he'd finished reading the scores. He lowered the paper and folded it in half, never taking his eyes off me. He looked dreamy, nostalgic. I wanted to hand over the receiver, but I held it tightly to my ear, listening to the promises my mother was making.

"We'll go to Europe," she was saying. "I think you're old enough now. It's been so long since I was there! I want you to see the beautiful churches, the museums. I'll take two—no three—weeks off. I think I can manage. We'll have the most wonderful time, just you and me."

My father was looking at me with an expression I didn't understand. He rose from his chair and walked over. His chest loomed in front of me. Then one of his big thumbs pressed against my cheekbone and slipped across my face.

"Don't cry," he said softly.

"I miss you, darling," my mother said. "Call me collect whenever you want. I'll write you soon. I'll plan our trip."

My father walked to the sliding glass door and stood watching Bonnie, who was squatting among the dead daffodils. I said goodbye to my mother. Without looking back, Dad opened the door and strode across the patio, stopping briefly at the edge, as if he were about to wade into a freezing stream. The grass was long, it was new spring grass, and the cold blades must have cut into his bare feet like sharp little knives.

He walked to Bonnie and stood over her, telling her something I couldn't hear. She sat on her heels and squinted, shielding her eyes from the sun with one gloved hand. The other held a bunch of flowery weeds—delicate yellow blossoms at the end of long stems. She held them as if she were gathering them to put in a vase, but then tossed them behind her into a mound of weeds she'd already pulled.

She gave my father a shrug and went back to her gardening. He turned and stared down at the lake. The clouds were racing. His hair blew forward. The sun must have been hot on his back, attracted by his navy blue shirt, but the wind was cold, blowing from the north. A perfect spring mix of hot and cold, like water from two faucets combining in the sink. These were my father's last days. Everything seemed normal, or a little bit better. No fighting or yelling, no bad weather, no skinned knees or flu. I was ashamed of my tears but I didn't stop crying. Before anyone else saw me, I ran up to the bedroom, opened the door and nearly tripped over Kitty's plastic horses. Kitty wasn't there but she'd left the horses arranged in a large circle, all facing the stallion, who was rearing in the center.

✢ ✢ ✢

My father loved parties. For his going away, Bonnie invited neighbors and Dad's colleagues and students from the deaf institute. Ralph Richards, a pitcher who had played with Dad and now lived in Spartanburg, said he'd drive up with his wife and two kids.

My father had just received his assignment: boot camp in Fort Rucker, Alabama. The army didn't want him to go to Vietnam. They said he'd be more useful behind a desk in Hawaii. But he was determined to get to the fighting. None of us doubted that he would.

For the party I wore a pair of navy blue bell bottoms covered with large white stars. My shirt was red and white striped. I tied my hair back with a thick piece of red yarn.

Bonnie laughed when she saw me. "Your father will love it."

Just before the guests arrived, Dad arranged us under the streams of twisted crepe paper and took Polaroids—single portraits as well as group shots. In one we wore hats and masks. Bonnie put on a rubber cat nose with whiskers, I wore Groucho Marx glasses, and Raymond and Kitty pulled out their old Halloween masks.

"I'll take these with me," Dad said. He set the pictures on the counter by the *hors d'oeuvres* that Bonnie and I had spent all afternoon making. I had scooped melon balls and filled celery sticks with peanut butter while Bonnie molded cheese into a ball covered with walnuts. The cake, which we'd ordered from the Greek pastry shop, was covered in army green frosting, with toy soldiers and palm trees lining the edges. It said, in black letters, "Hurry Home Dad."

A group of Dad's high school students were the first to arrive. If not for Dave Brubeck playing on the stereo, the room, filled with people, would have been totally silent.

The neighbors arrived, some carrying presents, not for Dad, but for Bonnie, in order to console her: a dish towel with a rabbit pattern, an arrangement of dried flowers. Several had chipped in and bought her a blender. The kids, seizing the Halloween masks, chased each other through the yard. The men dipped into the cooler of Old Milwaukee beer or poured mixed drinks at the bar. Dad told a story (making sure the students could see his lips and hands) about his uncle in Korea, who had been a doctor in a MASH unit. The students laughed at odd places, like foreigners watching a movie in subtitles.

When Bonnie introduced me as Hank's oldest daughter, people smiled in a puzzled way. I felt like an old doll dragged out of the toy chest. "What interesting trousers," one lady said to me. I recognized her from church, wearing the same straw hat with a band of fake flowers.

I stationed myself beside the *hors d'oeuvres*, in case they needed replenishing. I ate a piece of celery and looked at the photographs. They would have been perfect had it not been for me. Bonnie, Dad, Kitty and Raymond all fit together, resembled each other—a perfect family. And there I was, trying somehow to fit in. My clothes were too bright. My teeth were crooked. I didn't resemble anyone, not even my father, and I wished I'd worn the Groucho Marx glasses in every shot.

Mrs. Leonard, our neighbor, walked up to the counter and examined the deviled eggs. She gave me a sidelong glance, pinched an egg and nibbled at the white. "Faye, honey," she said, a touch of yolk on her upper lip. "Run get me a napkin."

"Yes, ma'am." I went behind the counter and grabbed a stack, trying to fan them as Bonnie had done.

"Never mind that," Mrs. Leonard said. "Just hand me one, sweetie."

She dabbed her orange lips with the corner of the napkin, then popped the rest of the egg in her mouth. She giggled and licked the tips of her long fingers.

"My goodness, Faye," she said after she'd swallowed.

Had I been staring? I looked quickly down at the counter. I tried again to twirl the napkins but somehow they flew out of my hands and fluttered to the kitchen floor.

Mrs. Leonard helped me pick them up. "I think they're fine," she whispered, scrunching her nose. "We just won't tell anybody they touched the floor."

From the living room came the sound of piano chords and Dad's trumpet case snapping open. I reached behind Mrs. Leonard to pick up a napkin. Her powder blue dress was stretched tightly across her hips and thighs. The heels of her feet had risen out of her dyed-to-match pumps.

"You must be sad, with your Daddy going off." Her face was so close, I smelled the egg on her breath. "You came all this way to live with him and now he's going off."

"Yes, ma'am," I said, trying to be polite.

"What does your momma think?" she continued, ignoring the music. We remained squatting on the floor. I reached for a napkin, moving away from her. "Him going to Vietnam. Isn't your momma—" She paused and I looked up into her eyes, which also matched her dress. "Isn't your momma a liberal?" She pronounced the word as if she'd meant to say "criminal."

In the other room people were snapping their fingers and clapping. I rose from the floor without answering Mrs. Leonard. A bald man in a gray sweat suit was playing the piano, a small green parrot perched on his shoulder. My father's right foot kept time with the music, rising and falling with exaggerated motion. His students kept their eyes glued to his foot and tapped along with him.

Bob Leonard, Mrs. Leonard's husband, was across the room, his arms around two of the deaf students. I wondered how the two of them could possibly be married. Mr. Leonard wore his pants so low they threatened to fall off. His untrimmed beard jutted out in clumps. He taught high school chemistry and, according to Dad, kept up with the latest in music and books. Sometimes he and my father played pool at Schiller's Pub, over Mrs. Leonard's objections.

I wanted to leave her and join the crowd around the piano, but she stood up and handed me a few napkins. She fingered the piece of yarn in my hair. The way she tickled my cheek, with just the tips of her long fingernails, made me think suddenly of my mother. A shiver ran down my spine.

"But you." She smiled at the stars on my pants. "You're just like your daddy. Red, white and blue."

She was waiting—I didn't know what for. My eyes were glued to the blue field of her dress, which contained little nubs of linen. I felt like picking them off, as I would balls of wool on a sweater.

"Faye, sweetie, you *are* a strange child." Her lips were pressed together with impatience, deepening the creases on both sides of her mouth.

Suddenly I could picture her teeth—long and white like her fingers, like fingers without flesh, a mouth full of bones.

"But then," she mused, "you come from a family of eccentrics."

If I didn't get away from her, I was going to say something terrible. I might come right out and say, "Fuck off." She was leaning over me like a giant bird about to peck. I wished my father would look at me or call, but he couldn't speak while he was playing. His cheeks blossomed out, as if the trumpet were filling *him* with air. I remembered what he had once called Mrs. Leonard after coming home from Schiller's Pub, his pockets filled with money he'd won playing pool. "Old pointy tits," he'd called her, sticking his fingers inside his shirt, pointing them out and wiggling them till Bonnie and I had laughed.

I looked straight at Mrs. Leonard and imagined myself saying the same thing, sticking my fingers inside my shirt and wiggling them in her face.

She drew herself up and frowned at me. She walked to the bar and picked up a bottle of gin. Annoyed, she gazed at the teaspoon of liquid remaining in the bottle. Then, with a sigh, she instead opened the vodka and splashed it straight over ice. As she took a swallow, she looked at me so strangely I had to think twice. Had the words actually come out of my mouth?

"Faye." It was Bonnie, calling me. "I need your help." She had appeared from nowhere and put her arm around my waist. Her perfume, different from what she usually wore, took my breath away.

I held the refrigerator door open as she slid out the cake. A couple of palm trees had fallen onto their sides, pitting the icing. The toy soldiers looked strangely out of place, then I realized why. They were from the Civil War, dressed in gray uniforms. They rode horses, aimed muskets and fired cannons.

"Bonnie, you've run out of gin." Mrs. Leonard tapped the empty bottle with her fingernails.

"Oh dear," Bonnie said and went to look in the liquor cabinet.

"It's perfectly all right," Mrs. Leonard said. "I've poured myself a vodka."

Mrs. Leonard returned to the counter, holding her tumbler up to the light. Then she leaned down close and gave me such a mean look, I thought she was going to pinch me.

Bonnie couldn't find another bottle of gin. "Who knows what people like to drink. Gin is depressing to me."

"This is a lovely party," Mrs. Leonard said. "I had no idea deaf people could be so musical."

"They can do lots of things. They're not stupid," I said.

Mrs. Leonard looked at me, taken aback. "You're a very strange child. Quite unpredictable."

Bonnie laughed and pulled me close, wrapping her arms around me. "Why, this child is as quiet as a mouse." She winked at me. "Her father and I have been encouraging her. We want her to speak up and have some fun."

She gave me a little push towards the music. As I passed the platter of deviled eggs, on impulse, I grabbed one. I stuffed the whole thing in my mouth and smiled. Bonnie laughed and Mrs. Leonard said, "Humph." I couldn't have spoken back if I'd had to.

☙ ☙ ☙

Though I knew the words to "When I'm Sixty-Four," I didn't want to sing. I didn't like my voice. My father was silent, too, and I remembered that he had never been able to carry a tune. He kept his trumpet close to his lips, even when he wasn't blowing it.

I stood next to a young deaf boy, about Kitty's age, whose head bobbed back and forth. He had licked all the salt off a pretzel he was holding. I smiled at him but we couldn't talk, not even to say each other's names. Unlike me, he wasn't shy about singing. His voice was loud but so uncontrolled that if I hadn't known the words to the song, I wouldn't have understood him.

The doorbell rang and Bonnie answered, welcoming some late arrivals. I turned and there, not ten feet away, stood the boy who liked me, Aaron Chandler.

Aaron's eyes lit up when he saw me. I had been avoiding him at school, purposely snubbing him, since his invitation to the ravine. Thank goodness we'd had no classes together. But I had run into him a couple of times in the halls and he had given me the same look he was giving me now—a wide-eyed stare that dripped with love and made me sick to my stomach.

I pushed past the little deaf boy, hurried to the kitchen and poured myself a Coke. My hands were shaking. I took careful sips before turning and stealing a glance at Aaron.

He had arrived with his parents. His father turned out to be Kitty and Raymond's pediatrician and his mother was a psychologist who sometimes counseled deaf students. Never, in my wildest dreams, had I imagined a connection between Aaron's parents and my father, though it was a small town where everyone knew everyone else.

Aaron wore a pair of bell bottom jeans and a mustard-colored Nehru jacket. A peace medallion hung from his neck. His parents seemed proud of him, despite these provocative ornaments, and pushed him along in front of them, introducing him to all their friends.

The room had filled with smoke. Aaron, like a specter, appeared and vanished, as if he were wandering through fog. Whenever I looked at him—I tried to keep track of him in order to stay out of his way—somehow he knew, and even if he was in the middle of shaking someone's hand, he returned my glance. It was only a matter of time before he cornered me.

"So *that's* Aaron," Bonnie whispered. Usually I appreciated her attempts at being my friend, but there were times when I wished she would ignore me.

"He's not so bad. He's kind of cute." She gave me a hopeful look.

"Ugh," I said.

She smiled and took a sip of wine, adding another pink lip print to the rim of her glass.

At that moment the Chandlers were making their way towards my father, who took the trumpet out from between his knees and shook Dr. Chandler's hand. I was pleased to see that Kitty and Raymond were also dismayed at the Chandlers' arrival, as if they imagined Dr. Chandler carrying two giant needles in his pocket.

My father kissed Mrs. Chandler on the cheek. She was the most fashionable woman at the party, and also the most scantily-clad. Her dress was split into two pieces, a top and a bottom, connected by giant plastic rings. Her bare white midriff showed. She wore chartreuse-colored stockings and her skirt, unlike those of the other women at the party, was above her knees.

When my father kissed her, she closed her eyes. One of her hands lingered at his elbow. Then she opened her eyes and gave my father a look that was fleeting but unmistakable.

The party seemed to stop for a moment. My father stared back at Mrs. Chandler, who leaned towards him, rocking forward onto the toes of her high heels as if she might lose control at any moment and throw her arms around him. His hands were poised, tight, ready to catch her if she fell.

They stood that way forever. Then Mrs. Chandler said something with her hands. As a counselor to the deaf students, of course, she knew sign language. What she said was brief, maybe three or four words. I couldn't understand the exact meaning but the tone was clear. She had touched her heart.

My father held out the palm of his hand, as if to say, "Be quiet." He smiled in a bland sort of way and patted Mrs. Chandler on the shoulder.

I looked all around the room. None of the guests seemed to have noticed. Dr. Chandler had turned his back on his wife and was mixing two martinis. Aaron stood with his hands jammed into his pockets. The minute I looked at him, he looked back.

I was afraid to look at Bonnie, who was standing right beside me. All evening she had been running back and forth between the guests and the kitchen. Now she was utterly still. I thought suddenly of how nice she had been to me—nicer, in fact, than my own father had been.

Finally I glanced up. Her eyes had a far-off look and she was smiling, relaxed, distracted from the party. At that moment, she looked prettier than ever. Her brown hair formed a heart shape around her head and neck. She was wearing a pair of tiny diamond earrings my father had given her that sparkled when she turned her head.

"I was thinking," she said, taking another sip of wine. "When your father leaves, and school lets out, why don't we all go camping? Just because he's gone doesn't mean we can't have some fun, does it?"

"No," I said, to please her. In principle, it was the right attitude—to buck up and make the best of things. But we shouldn't have *too* much fun, at least not too soon.

"Your father actually suggested it," she said, as if to reassure me. "He wants us to go on with life. He says we mustn't wait for him."

"Do you think he's coming back?" Before I knew it, the words were out of my mouth.

Bonnie looked at me, startled. She put her hand on my shoulder and gave me a look of concern. "Of course," she said. "Don't you?"

She thought I meant, would he survive the war? But during the course of the party, I had almost forgotten he was going into the army. The scene between my father and Mrs. Chandler had raised another possibility. My father had been married three times already. What was to prevent him from meeting someone else, falling in love and disappearing again?

He had left Mrs. Chandler and walked over to the piano. He was saying something to his students, most of whom had loosened up considerably. Now instead of talking only with their hands, they were trying to sound out words. Dad was encouraging them.

He looked so innocent, I convinced myself I'd made a mistake. He wasn't paying any attention to Mrs. Chandler now, though she kept staring at him.

"Faye." Bonnie looked at me with a kind expression, which made me feel ashamed.

"I'd love to go camping."

"Faye, do you think your father will come back?"

"Yes," I said, suddenly happy, even giddy. If Bonnie, who was married to him, who knew him better than anyone, believed he would come back, why shouldn't I?

She let out a sigh of relief. "Well," she said, picking up an empty beer can from the coffee table. "That's settled." She surveyed the room and determined the guests to be ready. "Why don't we go cut the cake?"

✢ ✢ ✢

Too late I realized I'd let down my guard. As Bonnie walked away, Aaron leaped into action, making rapid strides across the room. I was trapped against the living room wall.

As he bore down on me, he appeared both slimmer and taller. Had he been on a diet? It might have been the cut of the Nehru jacket, which he'd never worn to school and which hid the roll of fat at his waist.

Suddenly the din of the party was overwhelming. It wasn't just the adults who had gotten drunk. Some of the students had sneaked a beer or two and the alcohol was making them wild. Their laughter was loud and unrestrained, in contrast to the polite chuckling of the hearing people.

It had grown dark outside. The spotlights shone down into the backyard. The ravine lay just beyond the light, like a moat at the boundary of our property. Bonnie had placed bowls of nuts on the patio to entice people out, but no one was braving the late April cold.

When I looked back, Aaron was in front of me, grinning. The other guests were making their way towards the dining room, where Bonnie was cutting the cake. Ralph Richards, the pitcher, cried, "Speech." This prompted others, like Mr. Leonard, to yell also.

Aaron smelled faintly like gasoline. I wondered if he'd been mowing the lawn before coming to the party, or if he'd filled up his parents' car with gas. He was probably old enough to drive, though only with a learner's permit. Soon he might have a car of his own. I myself dreamed of owning a maroon Mustang, which I hoped would appear in the driveway on my sixteenth birthday.

Aaron inched his way closer. He and I couldn't have been more conspicuous, standing alone in the living room. More than anything, I wanted to escape from him and weave my way into the crowd. Instead I squeezed myself between the wall and the end table and finally, with exaggerated nonchalance, sat down on the arm of the sofa.

He sat right down beside me.

My father was agreeing to make a speech. He took a few steps up the circular stairway in the foyer, until he was above the crowd. He bowed his head as if composing himself and waited for the guests to be quiet.

Aaron pressed his arm against mine. The skin beneath my sleeve prickled. Neither Aaron nor I said a word. The small bright spot of interest I'd felt in him because he could drive vanished the minute he touched me.

I longed to be one of the crowd. I thought of offering to get Aaron a piece of cake, just as an excuse to leave him. But something kept me from moving, even from moving my lips to speak.

Then it was too late. My father lifted his head to begin his speech and I was stuck where I was. It seemed as if the lights had dimmed, all except a spotlight on him. Everyone else in the room was floating in a sort of half light that robbed them of color and disguised their faces and gestures. Aaron and I, in another room altogether, were virtually in darkness.

"When I was a boy," my father began, "I wanted to go to war. As some of you know, my father was a colonel. He himself survived three wars."

It was hard to believe he was talking about my grandfather, who had been helpless without his wife—couldn't make his own breakfast or go to church—and who used to fall asleep in his recliner listening to baseball on the radio. My mother had occasionally taken me to visit them, even after my father left, at their house not far from ours in Atlanta. But one day my grandmother, in a freak accident, got hit by a car as she was crossing the road. Not long afterwards my grandfather died in his sleep.

I'd never heard my father talk about his father and I waited for what he would say next. Everyone else in the room waited, too. Someone cleared his throat. My father was pausing an awfully long time, his right hand frozen in the shape of his last word—the outstretched fingers of "war." Clearly, he hadn't prepared his speech. I was afraid, for some reason, that, having invoked his father, he was seeing him, stern-faced and disapproving, in the corner of the room. He searched the faces in front of him. He searched for words, as if this speech were vital, as if he suddenly needed to explain everything—not only his decision to go to Vietnam, but every decision he'd ever made in his life.

At the same time Aaron stirred beside me, his elbow moving backwards, the sleeve of his Nehru jacket brushing against my arm. The friction caused an unpleasant sensation of heat to rush up my shoulder and neck.

My father opened his mouth but no words came out. Aaron's hand roved near my leg. I felt on the brink of disaster. Then Aaron's fingers wormed their way beneath mine and suddenly he was clutching my hand.

That's when my father's voice returned. I strained, trying to listen. But my body—every atom of my physical being—was concentrated in the palm of Aaron's hand.

I swallowed, knowing I couldn't let Aaron keep holding my hand, because it was unbearable. There was absolutely no pleasure in it, and yet, at the same time, I was thrilled.

Dad's deep voice boomed out. I couldn't resist him either—the black concentration of his eyes, the mysterious, graceful language of his hands. He talked about becoming a man. He said he had searched for ways to do this all his life—through team sports, through music, through the solitude of riding across snowy fields in pursuit of a few lost sheep. But he hadn't faced death, and this, he said, was what all his experiences had led to.

I had the strange feeling that I'd never really looked at my father. His eyebrows gave a slight upward turn where they tapered off near his temples. His earlobes clung tightly to his neck. I noticed these various, separate details but even more striking was the overall picture he presented to me. He was the handsomest man I'd ever seen.

"For me this war isn't about Communism," my father was saying, "though it's true my country needs me." His students were rapt and I wondered if he made a practice of talking to them about his experiences. Even Mrs. Leonard was listening, her chin tilted up, perhaps even trembling a little.

Aaron squeezed my fingers. A few seconds later, he squeezed them again. He wanted some response—for me to look at him or give him a squeeze back. It was too much to ask. I gathered my courage and with a mighty yank, pulled my hand away.

"I'll miss you all," my father said. "You don't know how much I'll miss you."

Aaron breathed heavily beside me. I couldn't make myself look at him. My father's face had the same dreamy expression I'd seen once before, when he'd overheard me talking to my mother.

Bonnie was still in the dining room, with Kitty leaning against her. What surprised me was the expression on her face. Her brow furrowed and Kitty began to squirm, trying to get out of Bonnie's grasp. For a moment I couldn't figure out what Bonnie was feeling. Then it hit me. She was angry.

I followed her angry stare, which came to rest not on my father, but on Mrs. Chandler, who was standing near the front door, holding her martini glass by the stem. It was slowly tipping and spilling. Her right hand, adorned with a large aquamarine, lay flat against her chest. Tears streamed down her face and when the gin hit her shoe, a loud sob escaped from her. Several people in the room turned and stared, everyone, in fact, except the deaf people.

I didn't dare look at Aaron though suddenly I felt sorry for him. For some reason, I remembered the first time I'd seen him and found out who he was. It was the week before he invited me to the ravine. He'd been doing his Joe Cocker imitation. A few ninth graders had gathered into groups in the courtyard. I was talking to Gina, a girl who was the object of envy and fascination because she owned a horse. But I had one ear on Aaron, who was laughing loudly on the other side of the courtyard.

There was something sleazy about his laugh. Sleazy and knowing and rebellious.

"Aaron," Gina had said, turning up her nose. Then with a sneer she had whispered, "He's Jewish."

At the time I hadn't thought much about her remark. I had sneered along with her, not because Aaron was Jewish, but because he was an easy target. When he had sung, in a voice that echoed off the walls, "I get high with a little help from my friends," Gina and I had doubled over, with laughter and disgust.

Now I was ashamed to have let Gina's remark pass. It wasn't just because of how Aaron's mother was acting. I wished I'd defended Aaron from the start.

I turned now to look at him, expecting him to be mortified. But he was watching his mother, one eyebrow raised, the hint of a smile around his mouth. What was he feeling—tolerance, amusement? Anyone in his right mind would have been embarrassed.

My father took a step down, towards Mrs. Chandler. Across the room, Bonnie took a step forward. I thought there might be a confrontation. I thought Bonnie might punch Mrs. Chandler or pull her hair. What a relief when my father walked past Aaron's mother—she turned her head slowly, her eyes followed him across the room—and headed straight for Bonnie. Someone started to clap. The sound was abrupt and sharp, like a shot in the midst of so much silence. It was one of my father's students, who hadn't heard Mrs. Chandler gasp. The student clapped his hands above his head, encouraging the other students to join him. By the time my father reached Bonnie and bent down to kiss her, everyone was clapping.

✢ ✢ ✢

After the party ended late Friday night, and before Sunday morning when my father left for Fort Rucker—that thirty-six hour period—Bonnie, the children, and even my father, all moved about in a daze.

Dr. Chandler had whisked his wife and son out of the house immediately after Dad's speech. His strategy was, I suppose, to avert further scandal by removing his wife from the scene. A more effective tactic would have been to stay and act as if nothing had happened. By leaving immediately he confirmed everyone's suspicions: my father and Mrs. Chandler were having an affair.

Or were they? I suspected not. But I imagined that Mrs. Chandler—Judith was her name—had on several occasions entered my father's office, shut the door and pleaded with him to love her.

What made me think it was so one-sided? Partly wishful thinking, but also observation of the way my father had treated Mrs. Chandler. He hadn't completely ignored her, which would have made me suspicious. The kiss he had given her had been no different from the kisses he'd given to other women at the party. And though Mrs. Chandler had tried to attract his attention by staring and wearing an eye-catching dress, he had remained indifferent. And finally, even after she'd tried to say something to him in sign language, he had held out the palm of his hand, a gentle way of saying, No.

After the Chandlers had left the party, I'd overheard bits of conversation. "Psychologists are always unstable," one lady had said, and I would have believed her—her theory of "it takes one to know one" made some sense—but her tone of voice was vicious. I heard more than one person accuse Judith Chandler of being a Yankee, a women's libber and a Jew. The lady in the straw hat had even said something about Aaron. "Allowing her son to wear a peace medallion!" she had said to Mrs. Leonard.

Actually I couldn't have cared less what the old birds said. I was upset because Bonnie, whose composure I had always admired, whose happiness I had taken for granted, had become quiet and morose. It was an effort for her to clean the house the morning after the party. She moved slowly from room to room and sometimes on her way to the kitchen, she stopped, her hands full of empty glasses or overflowing ashtrays, and began to cry. Later, after the house was clean, she made blueberry muffins for breakfast. Though all of us proclaimed in loud voices how delicious they were, she barely smiled and wouldn't eat with us.

I didn't know what I could do to persuade her that my father was innocent, but I had to find a way. I remembered the look on Aaron's face—of tolerance or amusement—and was convinced he had the answer.

But the question was, Did I have enough time? Would Bonnie believe the truth if it were presented to her? Or, failing that, would she soften and forgive my father before he had to leave? I was convinced their marriage was at stake. On the one hand, I felt helpless to intervene. I was young and my track record wasn't good: I hadn't been able to save my own parents' marriage. On the other hand, I felt an inexplicable loyalty to Bonnie and there was a part of me that said, Here is your opportunity to show your appreciation, to show how much you love them. I resolved to do everything I could to keep their family together.

My mission launched me into a frenzy of activity. I set several wheels in motion. I made outlandish promises to Raymond and Kitty, invited them to Atlanta and offered to take them to a Braves game and to Six Flags if they promised to be good for the next twenty-four hours. I called my mother and asked her questions I'd never asked before. Did she think I was pretty? Was I smart? Was it possible for boys to like me?

She answered in soft, amused yes's, as I had known she would. She asked what was up, but I said, "Nothing," and she didn't press me further.

I was ready to make my final move. From an upstairs phone I dialed Aaron Chandler's number. If he hadn't answered the phone I would have hung up, but I was lucky. He did. When I identified myself, he was quiet for a moment, probably flustered and surprised. But it was nothing compared to the surprise he must have felt when I invited him to the ravine.

✢ ✢ ✢

On my way out the back door (having made up a story about horseback riding with Gina, which, surprisingly, didn't raise an eyebrow. Why had I thought that Dad and Bonnie would expect all of us to stay home the day before my father left?), I remembered a Ray Bradbury story I'd once read about a ravine. In the story, evil spirits floated up from the ravine at night. Lost, frightened people disappeared down into it. The story had scared me and I regretted having read it. But how was I to know that one day I would venture down into such a place?

It was mid-afternoon, another perfect day. The sun was warm, the air was cold and there were lots of small puffed clouds floating in the far reaches of the sky. I was wearing exactly what I would have worn had I really been going riding—jeans, boots lined with rabbit fur that my mother had given me for Christmas, and a plain green sweatshirt. I had tried to cover myself from head to foot and had even stuck a pair of gloves in my back pocket, to keep the poison ivy off my hands.

Of course I hadn't told Aaron what my real intentions were. I had said, in my most casual voice, "I thought I'd go down to the ravine this afternoon and maybe smoke a few cigarettes." He would bring the yellow joint he had shown me, but I would refuse to smoke that. A cigarette was a good compromise—illicit but not exactly a drug.

I hadn't come up with a plan for getting the information I needed, though I had rehearsed various ways of raising the subject. "Gosh, Aaron," I might say, "your mother really liked my father's speech." Or what about directly bringing up the subject of divorce? I could remind him that my own parents had separated, then say, "I don't have much faith in the institution of marriage. How about you?"

I was halfway hoping he would bring it up himself, that he would feel the need to explain. But I wasn't counting on that. How perfectly, how remarkably, he had retained his composure, even after his father had angrily snapped his fingers and motioned him towards the door. Aaron had stood and raised his hand towards me in a wave goodbye, which I hadn't had the wits to respond to, and only after he was gone had I realized that the entire time we were sitting next to each other, we hadn't said a word.

Part of me was horrified that we had held hands. As I walked down the street towards Gina's house (after half a block I would double back around and into the ravine), I tried to put Aaron out of my mind. But I knew he would try to hold my hand again, only this time we would be alone.

"He's not so bad. He's kind of cute." What exactly had Bonnie meant? Had she been trying to console me? Had she been giving her approval?

I assumed Dr. Chandler was a good pediatrician. Bonnie wouldn't have taken Raymond and Kitty to anyone incompetent. But where had the Chandlers lived before and what had caused them to move here? Maybe there had been a scandal. Was Judith Chandler the black sheep of some wealthy Northern family? Had Dr. Chandler gotten her pregnant fifteen years ago and been paid to marry her and take her far away? It was odd that Aaron was their only child—at least I hadn't heard of others. I started to feel almost sorry for Mrs. Chandler, wearing those chartreuse stockings, with her midriff showing. My mother had also worn skirts above her knees—it wasn't unusual for Atlanta women. Maybe Mrs. Chandler belonged in a city. Maybe she and my mother would have been friends, especially if what the ladies had said at the party was true, that she was a women's libber, a "liberal," as Mrs. Leonard might have put it.

That made me feel a little better about Aaron, but not much. I stopped, halfway down the street, and turned and looked at my father's house. Raymond and Kitty had come out into the street with a baseball and their mitts. Dad wasn't far behind. This would be the last time he would play catch with them. I would have given anything to have been sitting in the yard, watching, listening to him give them pointers, even putting on a glove myself. But being there with them, even at the periphery of their game, was no longer possible. Not because I was down the street and couldn't have turned back, couldn't have said, Oh, I changed my mind about horseback riding. It was something else, something out of my control.

My reasons for calling Aaron—to pump him for information about his mother and my father—suddenly seemed ridiculous. Even if his mother had fallen in love with my father, how would Aaron know? And even if he did know, why would he tell me?

I wanted more from Aaron than simply information. I could hardly breathe, thinking about the hideous thrill of Aaron's fingers squeezing mine, the needles that pricked all over my skin. I wanted him to hold my hand again.

I stepped off the street and into the Morgan's side yard. The Morgans hadn't shown up at the party, which meant they were out of town. As I crept through their yard, filled with dogwood trees which seemed to have bloomed overnight, I peeked up into one of their windows. I saw a living room exactly like ours, with the same floor plan and fixtures, similar rugs and chairs, only the Morgans had used different colors to decorate. Their sofa, which was green, was situated, just like ours, at a right angle from the fireplace, which was built of exactly the same cream-colored stone, with veins of rust running through. They had a foyer with a winding staircase, exactly like the staircase where my father had given his speech. For a moment I felt disoriented. I saw people in the living room—the man with the parrot on his shoulder, the Leonards, the Chandlers. I even saw myself—a girl dressed like the American flag, perched on the arm of the sofa—with Aaron in his Nehru beside me. I felt like I was re-living the party, only this time from the outside, like one of Dad's students, watching everyone's lips, unable to hear a sound.

I saw myself and Aaron, in the moment before he held my hand. It was almost as if, by magic, I was being given another chance. I could re-live the moment and change it in whatever way I pleased. I could get up from the sofa the minute Aaron sat down. I could turn to him and say, "Would you like a piece of cake?" I could be wearing a flowered linen dress, white slippers with half-inch heels, a pair of tiny diamond earrings. I could look into his eyes and smile, with perfect poise, perfect grace, and say, "How nice to see you, Aaron Chandler. How nice of you to come."

Or I could make the scene darker, more terrifying, much worse than it had been. Instead of Aaron holding my hand, I could make him kiss me. In front of everyone at the party, in front of Raymond and Kitty, who would giggle and squeal, in front of Bonnie and Mrs. Leonard, who would say, in all her smugness, "I told you that child was unpredictable." My father, at first not able to see, would stop his speech and peer over. He would step down from the stairs, the crowd parting for him as he passed. Finally he would stand in front of us. My mouth would be pressed so hard against Aaron's that my lips would be white and I wouldn't be able to breathe or tear myself away, even with my father watching.

I turned from the window and pushed the back of my hand hard against my mouth. I couldn't, at that moment, imagine a kiss except as something painful.

Suddenly, from down the street, came the sound of a shrill cry. I ran to the front of the Morgan's house and peeked through the leaves of their hedge. Kitty had somehow gotten injured. She was standing with my father, who had his fingers in her mouth, as if the ball had hit her and knocked out her teeth. Raymond had scampered after the ball down the other end of the street and was walking back, throwing it into his glove with a loud thwacking sound. My father removed his fingers from Kitty's mouth. There was blood on her shirt. She and my father started up the front walk, leaving Raymond behind. My father had his arm around Kitty's shoulders and Kitty leaned against him, burying her head into his waist. She wasn't crying out loud anymore but she made little whimpering sounds.

Raymond stood in the street, pounding his glove with the ball. He looked like a little black-haired cat, with his nose twitching and a devilish look on his face. He had thrown the ball at Kitty, thrown it straight at her mouth to hurt her. I had asked the children to try and behave but obviously they hadn't understood. How could I have explained to them that their whole future might be riding on the course of this day, their father's last day, that whether they were good or bad might be the deciding factor?

Raymond looked up at the clouds then threw the ball high in the air, teetering underneath it, getting a bead on it, then slapping his glove, as if it were a real pop fly. He threw the ball again and again, most of the time failing to make the catch but sometimes making it perfectly, with remarkable dexterity for a boy not yet five. I had seen him playing catch on several occasions, but never by himself, and never so well.

He stopped and turned, pricking up his ears. The ball was squeezed in his glove. I couldn't help smiling—he was a funny little boy, with a puggish face, a belligerent expression, but with eyes so blue and lashes so long, they looked like a girl's. He squinted and for a moment I thought he'd seen me. Instinctively, I moved back, to take better cover. He stepped forward and stooped, removing his hand from his glove, and pinched the brim of his cap. Down went his eyes, his knee slowly lifting—a perfect imitation of a wind-up. Then he threw the ball, a lovely arcing curve, what my father would have called a lollipop. It bounced on the pavement not far from where I crouched and Raymond gave chase down the street. I didn't give him a chance to discover me. I ran behind the Morgan's house, not looking back or stopping until I had launched myself into the ravine and lay there, breathing heavily, in the middle of a huge patch of poison ivy.

✢ ✢ ✢

The ravine was damp and musty, and at the bottom was a narrow creek. My sweatshirt wasn't nearly warm enough. I could see a hundred yards in either direction but there was no sign of Aaron. I realized I had forgotten to bring the half empty pack of cigarettes I'd found after the party.

The only sounds were the trickling of water and a high rustling of trees. I slid down the slope and when I reached the creek, I squatted and looked down. There was movement everywhere. A crayfish crept along the creek bed, which was covered with stones and bits of mica that glinted as the branches above swayed. A school of a dozen or so minnows bumped and nibbled against the remains of a tadpole, bloated, the color of blue ice.

The water hypnotized me. I stared without blinking at a whirlpool then dropped a dead leaf into the current. It got swept up like a helpless boat, circling faster and more tightly until it stood upright and gave one last pirouette before being sucked down.

"Aaron," I whispered.

I had left the house around one-thirty and told Aaron to meet me at two. I wasn't wearing a watch but I knew he was late. I pushed my way through the rhododendron branches that extended out over the creek. At one point, bushes completely blocked the path and I had to step onto stones that poked up out of the water. Some of the stones were slippery and loose. When I made it safely back to the bank, I rested for a moment and listened. Someone, or something, was watching me. I turned but there was no one behind me, only the ravine, which seemed to stretch back forever—a dark tunnel filled with dampness and cold. I hurried towards the lake, where I could sit in the sun.

A twig snapped behind me. I turned and there he was.

"You scared me," I said.

He looked different from the way he had looked last night. His eyes were swollen, his hair stuck out wildly, and unlike me, he wore bright colors—an orange shirt and purple corduroy pants.

He caught me by the elbow. I jerked my arm away. Run, said a voice inside me. Run. He leaned close to my face, his long curls crinkling against my cheek. My skin grew hot where his face nearly touched mine.

I turned and ran as fast as I could. Aaron dove for my leg and his fingers locked onto my ankle and both of us crashed face first in the dirt.

"What's the matter with you?" I sputtered, turning to face him.

"Look. You cut yourself." He reached up to my chin, brushing off a wet leaf, and wiped the underside of my jaw. On the tip of his finger was a tiny streak of blood.

I took off my glove, wet my finger with spit and cleaned the cut. "Is it still bleeding?" I asked, sticking out my chin.

"No. It's not very deep." He rolled onto his back and stared up at the trees. "Lie down. It's like looking at stars."

How could he be so nonchalant? I glanced up at the top of the ravine. The tree trunks were lined like the slats of a fence. I realized, with a jolt that made the hair on the back of my neck rise, that we were directly behind my father's back yard. How foolish I was! At any moment someone might come to investigate our noise. Why hadn't I thought of that? At least gone in the other direction?

I rose to my feet. "I have to leave."

He looked at me, puzzled. "Why?"

His face, from that angle, looked peculiar, like the face of one of those dolls made from socks, with textured gray skin and yarn curls.

"Don't go," he said. He knelt in front of me and reached again for my ankle. He pressed his thumb on the toe of my boot and squeezed the edges like a shoe salesman checking a fit.

"Nice boots," he said. Then, to my surprise, he plunged his hand right inside.

"Stop it," I said. "That tickles." In fact, it didn't tickle. His hand was hot and the more he pressed, the more I hated him touching my dirty, smelly foot. Before I knew it, he had slipped my boot off.

"You can't leave now," he said.

"Okay, okay." I hopped on my other foot, about to lose my balance. "I won't leave. Just let me go."

He cocked his head and narrowed his eyes. In spite of myself, I smiled. That's when he yanked my foot and I fell back with a thud that jarred me to the teeth.

He laughed and sat back, cross-legged. When I tried to get up, he shook his head and tightened his grip around my ankle.

Slowly he began to touch my foot. He pushed his thumb into my arch, worked his fingers up to the ball of my foot, then poked, as best he could, in between my toes. I stared at his face with a look of disgust, which only made him grin.

What had happened since last night? He was goofy, a clown. Why wasn't he quiet and romantic? Why was he touching my *feet*?

"This is reflexology," he explained, gouging my arch with his knuckle. "That spot corresponds to your liver."

"It hurts," I said, pulling my foot away.

"I'll tell you what," he said, crawling closer. "I'll give you a massage on your back."

"I don't want a massage."

"But it will feel good. I promise."

He touched my shoulder and when I didn't protest, he gently pushed me back. I lay in the dirt, perfectly stiff, as if looking at him had turned me to stone. He loomed over me and I closed my eyes, unable to bear, just inches away, the exaggerated features of his face.

I kept my eyes closed and counted backwards from ten. I only got to seven. Then I felt the stubble around his lips, which scraped against mine. His smell—no longer of gasoline—made me need to swallow. Either he'd used strong minty toothpaste or had recently sucked on one of those horrible breath mints.

No one had ever kissed me. What surprised me was how easy it was. Aaron must have worked out the movements ahead of time. His rhythm, after a few moments, was easy to predict—his lips pressed mine, he opened my mouth, stuck his tongue inside, then he closed my mouth, removed his lips, took a deep breath and started all over again. It was easy to follow, like the steps of a dance.

I let him kiss me as long as he wanted and didn't open my eyes till he stopped. The first thing I saw were the tops of the trees. I peeled my hands from the back of Aaron's shirt. They were stiff and cold, despite my gloves. I had no idea how much time had passed. It seemed both colder and darker, the light through the trees a deeper yellow, almost gold. I shivered and sat up.

"Tonight," Aaron whispered, "you can sneak out again."

"It's too cold."

"I'll bring a sleeping bag."

"No." I looked at him for the first time in what seemed like hours. His head, with his curls even wilder, seemed to have grown disproportionately large for his body. "Don't you understand?" I said, looking down at my white sock. "My father's leaving tomorrow."

"Oh," he said, looking off in the distance.

My lips felt puffy and in a moment of panic I wondered if too much kissing could harm them. Maybe they were bleeding, like my chin, without my even knowing. I touched them and looked at my fingers, relieved that they were clean.

"And what about you?" Aaron asked. "Are you leaving tomorrow?"

"No, I have to finish school."

He nodded. "Next year I'm going to Exeter. I'm leaving this town. I hate it." He was staring at the ground, his fingers absently plucking up grass. He turned and lay with his hands behind his head, looking up again at the trees. "I'm going to live in a city. Maybe New York, maybe San Francisco. Do you know where you're going to college?"

"No," I said.

"I'm going to Harvard. My uncles live in Boston."

I was beginning to relax again, listening to him talk. He had such definite ideas.

"That's where my mother is from," he added. At the mention of his mother, we looked at each other.

"My uncles are big in the anti-war movement. You don't know about that, I guess."

I shrugged. It was true, I didn't know what he was talking about, but I didn't want to admit it.

"Why is your father going?" he continued. "What does he think he'll prove? You should hear what people say about Vietnam."

He had propped himself on one elbow and was touching the ribbed waistband of my sweatshirt. Each time I felt the cold tips of his fingers, I shivered. I looked beyond him at my boot lying near the creek. It had tipped over and the top was partially submerged. The fur was matted and soaked.

"The women fight, just like the men. Even sometimes the children. They carry bombs."

Something plunked in the creek—a small fish or an acorn falling. Aaron lifted my shirt.

"Hey," I said. "Don't do that."

"What?" He looked up at my face. His hand crawled like a spider underneath my shirt.

I took a deep breath and sucked in my stomach, trying to keep it away from his hand. His touch paralyzed me and made me feel helpless. Unlike the kiss and the way he'd held my hand last night, this touch—on my bare skin and close to places no one had ever touched or seen—was terrifying and wrong. He murmured something I couldn't hear. It seemed like he was in a trance, making strange little "M" sounds, as if he were chewing on food.

"Aaron."

He didn't open his eyes. His hand slid across my skin. I needed to stop him but I didn't know how.

Finally I had to do something. "Everyone knows about your mother," I said.

His mouth stopped abruptly. He frowned up at me—a look more of puzzlement than disapproval. For some reason, it inspired me to even greater cruelty. "You should have heard what they were saying last night, after you left the party."

I could tell he half wanted to know and half wished I wouldn't go on.

"Everyone knows," I said. "She threw herself at my father."

Aaron didn't say anything. He looked at me sadly, as if *I* were the one who deserved pity. His expression infuriated me.

"And when everyone left, my father told the truth. He said he tried to keep your mother away. She pursued him for months. He told her to leave him alone. But your mother wouldn't. She wouldn't leave him alone."

Aaron turned his face to the ground, looking miserable. What, I wondered, had made me lie? I debated whether or not to apologize. Before I could say anything, he lunged at me. He buried his face in my chest. I cried out but that didn't stop him from clasping one of my breasts and frantically kissing it. I was horrified but felt I deserved to be touched in this way, for telling such hideous lies. I stared at the water in the creek without blinking. A stream of bubbles rose and popped, as if some desperate creature were trapped below. I stared and stared, my body perfectly rigid. Aaron moved from one breast to the other, desperately kissing them through my sweatshirt. He seemed both hungry and guilty. I felt I had no choice but to let him continue.

An eternity later, he looked up at me, his mouth hanging open. He touched my chin with his fingers. "You're bleeding again."

I wiped my chin with the back of my glove. The wool was scratchy against the open cut and when I brought my hand down, I saw tiny beads of blood caught in the dark weave.

A blue jay screamed. We both looked up and I was startled by the bird's purposeful stare. He seemed to be screaming directly at us and threatening to swoop down and peck at our faces. He repeated his alarm, until I had to put my fingers in my ears.

Aaron lifted his head, straining to reach my mouth again. He was relentless. With his hand behind my head, he brought my mouth down and this time, as he worked my lips open, he lay his hand flat on my breast and moved it in a circle. I resisted him in every way I could, but not enough to stop him. My lips were drawn tightly across my teeth. When he put his tongue inside my mouth, I tried to push it back out.

By the time he stopped, I felt chafed, worn down. He held my cheeks in his hands. His eyes had gone from being swollen to having deep, haunted circles beneath them. He said, in a plaintive voice, "Will you sneak out tonight?"

"No."

"Please," he begged, stroking my hair.

"No," I said, more emphatically.

"Why not?"

"Because."

"Why not?"

"Because!"

My effort to stand was violent, enough to throw him out of my lap. With only one boot, I ran. The blue jay screamed and swooped through the ravine. As I ran, I said to myself, I hate Aaron Chandler. I hate Aaron Chandler. I was crying, my chin was bleeding. Once I tripped over a stump and fell.

I ran towards the lake. When I emerged from the ravine beside the shore, the sun was setting with long, cold rays that would soon disappear behind the mountains. I looked behind me to make sure Aaron hadn't followed then collapsed against a tree. I leaned back and closed my eyes.

It was then that I realized the truth. All thoughts of Aaron vanished. I stared at the meadow between me and the lake and could almost see the imprint—where the grass had bent under the weight of bodies. A few weeks ago, my father had stood by the lake, recklessly playing his trumpet. Bonnie had run down the path to meet him, wearing her long white robe. Her dark hair hung to her waist. But Bonnie's hair wasn't long enough to hang to her waist, even when she left it uncurled.

I had watched the two of them so intently, but the whole time Bonnie's back had been turned towards me. Not once had I seen her face.

Now I knew—it hadn't been Bonnie. Judith Chandler had met my father that night. He had played for *her*, had slipped off her robe, had gathered her in his arms. It was she, not Bonnie, who had made him so wild, with her unearthly appearance and her gleaming white body which he had smothered and kissed in the grass.

I felt deeply and irrevocably sad. The whole world seemed to darken with my sadness. The entrance to the ravine was black, like the gaping mouth of some awful beast who had spit me out. The lake was gray and so were the mountains. There was no color left in the sky. I didn't know what I was going to do or how I would go back to the house. But of course I had to. My father was leaving. In a few hours I would say good-bye.

I remembered how Aaron had looked at me—as if *I* were the one to be pitied. He had known all along that my father and his mother were in love. I felt doubly ashamed—not just because of my cruelty to Aaron, but because the truth was humiliating and I'd been duped. I'd believed in my father, and he had betrayed me, and Aaron had known all along.

I looked down at my filthy clothes, my white sock now muddy and black. I had left one of the boots my mother had given me, ruined, by the creek. I had to go back and get it. But what if Aaron was still there? What if he'd taken it with him?

I started to cry again. I wished I'd never come to live at my father's house. I remembered the day my mother had given me the boots. It was a few days before Christmas. We were celebrating early because I was going to my father's. How awful I had been to leave her alone at Christmas! And this time I'd left her for almost two months. My chest felt like it would burst, I loved her and missed her so much. I tried to reassure myself by remembering her letters, by repeating the promises she'd made to me. I would have given anything to be leaving tomorrow, to be going back to her. It wasn't just that I'd hurt her. It was that every day the chances grew that she would learn to live without me.

I sank so deeply into misery that I turned, buried my face in the grass, and cried. I cried with loud abandoned sobs. I wanted my mother, like a baby. I pressed my face as hard as I could into the grass, which smothered my cries like a pillow. I called her, over and over, until the earth itself seemed to take pity on me and put its arms around me.

✧ ✧ ✧

I dragged myself home, not caring who saw me, but luckily no one did. I walked through the front door, which was always unlocked during the day, and went straight upstairs. Vague murmurs came from my father's den, where he had his desk and telephone and where he kept all his albums and stereo equipment. At this time of day Bonnie was usually in the kitchen. The house smelled like meat, a pot roast or a stew, something being slowly cooked all afternoon.

As I passed Raymond's bedroom, he looked up from where he was sitting on the floor, inspecting his marbles. Every day he did an inventory. He liked to see and touch the things that were his, just as Kitty liked to linger over her plastic horses, greeting them, touching them, somehow acknowledging each one.

Upstairs, I took a scalding shower. When I got out and dried myself, I looked for the poison ivy rash. It hadn't appeared but my skin was splotched from the hot water. I inspected my chin, which wasn't scratched but punctured, as if I'd fallen onto a thorn. I threw my socks, jeans and sweatshirt into the dirty clothes bin, then, on second thought, retrieved them. I rolled the dirty sock inside the cleaner one and stuffed everything, even my underwear, into the upper pocket of my suitcase.

It was good to be clean, to put on clean clothes. I lay down on my bed and considered reading. I was close to the end of *Hawaii*, for the second time, and normally I wouldn't have been able to put the book down. At home, I would have brought it to the dinner table—my mother let me read as I ate. But I looked at the book and knew I wouldn't finish it. I thought of the characters, whom I had loved, truly cared for, and known better than I had known anyone in real life. I had been gratified by their sacrifices. Their tragedies had filled me with a sense of sorrow and justice.

What childishness. It was silly to have believed in them, to have needed them as much as I had. They weren't *real*, they weren't tawdry and ragged and impossible to understand. I thought of my father and what he had done with Judith Chandler, and I felt angry again. I sat up and stared out the window. It was by now so dark outside that all I could see were surfaces, textures of darkness—the soft black of the sky, the reflective, almost metallic surface of the lake, the muffled, uneven darkness of the branches and leaves hovering over the ravine. My eyes could penetrate none of that darkness and if there were people outside, doing things they weren't supposed to, I couldn't see them.

Kitty appeared at the door. The left side of her mouth was swollen and she held a dripping bag of ice at her side. She walked straight to my bed and looked up at me, leaning to her right to show me her lips.

"Look at that," I said. "How did that happen?"

"I had to go to the hospital," she said.

"You did?" I said, playing along with her. I didn't believe she'd gone anywhere that afternoon.

She opened her mouth, which was obviously a painful procedure, and showed me inside where there was a deep black hole where her bottom left incisor had been. She shut her mouth and looked up at me, waiting for my comment.

"You lost a tooth."

"My Dad threw the ball and it hit me in the mouth."

My first instinct was to say, He's my Dad, too. Then I thought, it was Dad, not Raymond, who had injured Kitty.

"He didn't mean to," she added.

"Well, of course not," I said, noticing the small dark stain on the floor where water was leaking from the plastic bag she held. "Your ice bag is dripping," I said.

She climbed onto my bed and looked out the window. For a moment I wondered if *she'd* ever seen anything she hadn't been supposed to see. The melted ice dripped onto the bedspread. She put the bag to her lip.

She stared into her lap then raised her eyes to me. She had the same eyes Raymond had, and my father's black hair. I wondered if she thought of me as her sister. I wondered if anyone had ever talked about me before my first visit, last Christmas. I had brought her a doll, which my mother had helped me pick out, a plain baby doll with a white lace dress. Kitty hadn't liked it. She played only with horses, or occasionally with the strange little trolls, which I thought were ugly. She stuck pins in their earlobes for earrings and braided their fluorescent orange and green hair. They occupied the shelf below the horses' and came in several sizes, one small enough to fit on the end of a pencil.

When I first moved into her room, the baby doll was propped against the pillow on my twin bed. Probably Bonnie had put her there, out of consideration to me. There wasn't a sign of wear on the doll. Her dress was perfectly white. Her eyes clicked open and shut, according to gravity, and when I asked Kitty what she'd named her, she said, "Sully." I was sure Kitty didn't know what the word meant, but she probably knew that it wasn't a nice thing to name a doll.

She was regarding me now with what seemed like skepticism. "Did you really go riding today?" she asked.

For a moment I panicked. What if Bonnie had called Gina's house and found out I'd never been there? I frowned and said, "Kitty, that bag is dripping all over my bed."

She gave a great sigh. "It's just water," she said.

"It's getting my bed wet."

She climbed down and disappeared into the bathroom, which joined her bedroom to Raymond's. I heard the bag of ice chunk against the sink. I could see the backs of her legs from where I sat. She was on tip toe, trying to look at her face in the medicine chest mirror.

"Remember how you told us to be good today?" she called out from the bathroom.

"Yes."

"Well, we were." She peeked around the corner of the door. She gave me a strange look, as if to say, Raymond and I behaved today. What did *you* do?

"You would have liked the horse I rode," I said. "He was completely black."

"What was his name?"

Tricky child. I had to think quickly. "Napoleon," I said, which was the first name that came to me. "He was black except for a white star on his forehead." I didn't know what impulse made me elaborate. Lies were best left simple.

She walked back into the room, reached into her pocket and held out her hand. In the center of her palm was the tooth she'd lost, a hard yellow kernel with a sharp tip. She turned it over and I saw the dark hole where the tooth had been connected.

"How much do you think I'll get?" she asked.

"From the tooth fairy?"

"Yes." She held the tooth between her fingers and made little puncture marks on the underside of her arm. "Feel it," she said and pushed the tip into the skin of my arm.

"Ow," I said and she smiled. "Did you know," I asked, "that you're going to lose all your teeth?"

She opened her eyes wide.

"Your front teeth and even the big ones in back."

"That's not true," she said.

"Yes, it is. And sometimes the teeth don't grow back. There was a girl at my school whose front tooth didn't grow back. She had to get a gold one."

Kitty looked disgusted. "Did you get all your teeth back?" she asked.

"What do you think?"

"Do you have a lot of fillings?"

"No."

"Let's see."

I opened my mouth and she peered inside. "You only have two," she said and reached back into my mouth to touch one of my molars. I bit down softly on her finger and she laughed. "Let go," she cried.

I loosened my jaw and she pulled her finger out. "Do you believe in the tooth fairy?" she asked.

I considered several things before answering. First that she was testing me, that someone had told her that the tooth fairy wasn't real and she was trying to get corroboration. Then I thought about how old she was, nearly seven, and realized she had probably lost many of her baby teeth already. It didn't seem possible that this little incisor was her first.

She had balled up her fist, with the tooth inside, and rested it on my knee. My stomach growled. What was keeping dinner? I looked out the window but it was so dark that all I could see were our reflections, Kitty's and mine.

Kitty was still waiting for me to answer. I touched the curls near her ear and she smiled. Then she did something she'd never done before. She crawled up onto the bed and put her head against my chest and wrapped her little arms around me. I was startled but it didn't take me long to respond, to hold her softly against me.

"No," I said, deciding upon the truth. "The tooth fairy is really your mother."

She let go of me and smiled. "I know," she said. "Do you want to come help me set the table? We're eating in the dining room tonight."

"It's Dad's last dinner."

"Until he comes back from the war," she corrected me.

"That's right. Till he comes back."

"You won't be here," she said with no trace of emotion. She was just stating the facts.

"No," I said. "I'll be back in Atlanta."

"Since we were good today," she said, "can we still come to visit you? Will you take us to a baseball game? Will we stay with your mother?"

"It depends," I said, "on how good you are tonight."

She rolled her eyes. "I'm *always* good," she said as if she were tired of behaving and wanted to be bad just once. "Raymond's the one who's not."

"Was Raymond bad today?" I asked, suddenly curious as to what had happened at the house while I was gone this afternoon.

"No, not bad," she said. "But he wanted to go to the hospital with us and Mom wouldn't let him."

She was persisting with this hospital story. Maybe it was true. "Dad took you?" I asked her.

"Yes. Mom said if he didn't, she was going to."

"Which hospital?"

"The one down the road." She pointed to her right. "Dr. Chandler gave me a shot with a big needle." She stuck out her tongue. "I hate him," she said.

Now I believed her. She was waiting for me to react, to scold her perhaps for using the word "hate," which I had heard Bonnie once reprimand her for, saying, "Hate is a strong word. It could hurt someone's feelings." But I didn't care if she hated Dr. Chandler or even if she had told him to his face. I was trying to think of a subtle way to phrase my questions, to find out what Dad and Dr. Chandler had really said to each other.

"What kind of shot did he give you?"

She shrugged.

"Was Dad there?"

"Yes."

"Did Dr. Chandler say anything to him?"

She stopped and considered. Something about the hospital visit had been unpleasant for her. But of course. She had been in pain. She'd been given a shot. Hospitals were frightening places no matter what.

"He said I would be just fine," she said.

"That's all?" I could hardly keep the excitement out of my voice. "He didn't say anything else? He didn't mention the party last night?"

"Maybe," she said softly. She put her finger on her nose and concentrated. Then she looked up at me. "No," she said. "I don't think so. I don't think he said anything about the party."

"Not even thank you?"

"No. Dad said thank you for taking care of me."

Maybe she didn't want to tell me, or she had been in such shock that she really didn't remember. But they had said *something* and she had heard it. I could tell by the way she was frowning and playing with the tooth she'd lost.

"Kitty!" Bonnie called up the stairs. "I thought I asked you to help me set the table."

Bonnie's voice was so cross that Kitty and I looked at each other and jumped off the bed. "I'll help you," I said, now completely dreading dinner. We might as well have invited the Chandlers, all three of them, to eat Dad's last meal with us. That's how unpleasant it was going to be.

"We'll both be good tonight," I said to Kitty. She nodded and we started downstairs.

✣ ✣ ✣

The dining room table was too beautiful to touch. We were eating from the china Bonnie had inherited from her mother—a blue and white pattern that looked Oriental—and drinking from crystal goblets. The silver had been polished so thoroughly you could see tiny scratches in the dips of the spoons. In the center of the table was a footed ceramic bowl piled with apples, pears and grapes.

I had eaten in the dining room only once before, last Christmas when I'd come for my first visit. The room was situated at the front corner of the house. It looked onto the street and the narrow front lawn with its curved driveway and trimmed hedges, lit by the front porch light. Windows, cracked open, lined two of the walls. They were old-fashioned sash windows with weights that rang like bells somewhere deep inside the walls every time you opened or closed them. Bonnie's parents had bought the house before she and her sisters had been born. Except for the two years she'd spent at college in Chapel Hill, Bonnie had never lived anywhere else.

Once when Bonnie and I had been driving the dogs to the vet's, she had pointed out the apartment where my father had lived before they were married. It was a beige cinder block building alongside a four-lane highway with motorcycles parked in front and a Tastee Freeze on the corner. The place was so squalid, with a dumpster overflowing with trash and no trees or hedges for decoration, that for a moment I didn't believe my father had lived there. But Dad had never been good with money. In fact, the three women he'd married had come from well-to-do families, with inherited money or property. Even Bonnie, after her parents died, had inherited this house and its contents.

I had wanted to ask Bonnie how the two of them had met. I had assumed it was after my father started working at the deaf institute. But now, after having seen my father with Judith Chandler, I wondered, for the first time, if he had met Bonnie while he was still married to my mother.

At the time of my parents' divorce, my father had been playing with his jazz band, the Caterpillars, on weekend nights at a club. I had never been there: the run-down shack near the Greyhound station in Atlanta that sold bottles of beer for a quarter. The clientele was mostly black, with an occasional group of students from Emory.

My mother, at that time, had been attending law school, staying up late, often at the library. One night my parents fought about my mother's study group, which consisted of five men and her, and with whom she spent a great deal of time. When my father left for good, several months later, my mother said, "Your father was so jealous. Maybe if I hadn't spent so many nights studying…"

But what if Bonnie had lured my father away? Maybe one of her high school friends had gone to Emory and on a visit to Atlanta, Bonnie had gone to the jazz club and been seated (because she and her friend were pretty and young) at one of the tables up front. There was my father, a slightly older man with dark eyes and pale skin, playing his trumpet, his hair falling into his face, his eyes closed except when he opened them and saw Bonnie. After the set, he came and sat at her table. The next night Bonnie sneaked out and took a taxi to meet him. They sat together in the back of the club, holding hands. My father smoked cigarettes. Bonnie was demure, eyes downcast, her left hand playing with the silver pearl pendant she still sometimes wore around her neck.

I remembered how much I had grown to love Bonnie over the two months I'd lived with her. I tried to recapture some of that feeling. But now, when I looked at her, sitting at the opposite end of the table, she didn't seem like the same person. It was hard to believe how much she had changed in just twenty-four hours. I wouldn't have called her pretty anymore. Her skin was gray; her eyes were red. She was wearing a dress I didn't like. It was brown with a white lace collar and made her look like one of the Puritans in my history book.

We ate in complete silence. Raymond, sitting next to me, speared his green beans, one at a time, with total concentration. Kitty got tears in her eyes when she chewed. She gave me a look across the table, a look full of pain, her pupils large and dark.

I was beginning to think that Bonnie and Dad would never speak to each other again. Dad cut into his roast, then put the knife down, an ebony-handled steak knife with tiny serrated teeth, and transferred his fork to his other hand. Even though he was chewing with his mouth closed, I could hear the food being ground down and swallowed.

The meal seemed to go on forever. The meat was making me sick—it was bloody, the juice laden with rainbowed pools of grease. Aaron had mentioned that his family was vegetarian. I pictured their dinner—lots of bright hot vegetables with butter melting on top.

"Bonnie," my father said, his face neutral and pleasant. "Would you please pass the jelly?"

Bonnie gave the saucer a violent push. The jar teetered then fell, dripping thick orangish-brown liquid onto the tablecloth. I picked it up and handed it to Dad.

"Thank you," he said, giving Bonnie a stern look. He spooned the jelly onto his bread plate.

Outside the dogs started to bark in their pen. Bonnie had been glaring at my father but abruptly she got up from the table, leaving her napkin beside her plate. It was so crumpled it would have taken a sizzling hot iron to make it smooth again. She had been squeezing it with all her strength.

"Excuse me," she said to Dad.

He looked up innocently and watched her leave the room. Nothing changed; none of us spoke. We ate our food with the same good manners and waited for her to come back.

The sound of her voice came through the open window. She was talking to the dogs. I couldn't make out the words, but the tone was the kind a mother would use with her babies. Dad looked out the window. A car drove slowly down the street. Though I couldn't see the driver through the car's tinted windows, I believed, for some reason, that it was Judith Chandler.

My father didn't give the slightest reaction to the sight of the car. It rolled down the street without stopping, then, with a flicker of its red brake lights, quietly turned and disappeared.

When Bonnie came back, her cheeks were pink and her hair stuck up in different directions. My father looked surprised, as if he hadn't believed she was going to come back at all.

Kitty said, "Mommy, your food is getting cold."

"What was the matter with the dogs?" Dad asked, his voice carefully modulated.

Bonnie didn't answer. Instead she looked at me. "Faye," she said in a sickly sweet voice. "How was riding this afternoon?"

I gulped down my beans. They seemed to turn sideways and stick halfway down my throat.

"Fine," I said, reaching for my water.

"Did you go on a trail or stay in the ring?"

I drank half the contents of my goblet. The beans washed down. "Trail," I managed to get out.

Bonnie raised one eyebrow. "I didn't realize you were that good a rider," she said without a smile.

"Her horse was called Napoleon," Kitty piped up.

I looked at Kitty and for the first time thought, this little girl *is* my sister. She smiled at me, as if she had knowingly come to my rescue, though I still wasn't off the hook.

"Napoleon," Bonnie said, staring at Kitty then turning to me. "Is that one of Gina's horses?"

Instead of answering, I looked at her and for a split second considered making a full confession. I looked at Dad, too. He was staring down into his plate, completely absorbed in eating.

Bonnie pushed the beans around in circles on her plate. I thought she might take pity on me. But when she asked her next question, I had no more doubts. She was trying to catch me in a lie.

"What was the name of Gina's horse?" she asked. "Doesn't she have a fine new horse?"

I nodded, taking a wild guess. Gina hadn't said anything about a new horse, but it was entirely possible she had bought one without telling me. I looked down at the pattern in my plate and thought of the name "Marco Polo" for her horse, but I didn't answer Bonnie. Without thinking, I touched the scab on my chin.

"What's that?" Bonnie asked.

"It's nothing."

"You hurt yourself," she said. "How did you hurt yourself?" She was cutting a piece of meat and stirring her mashed potatoes. She kept looking from her plate to my face. I was struck dumb. Minutes seemed to pass, during which my mind was totally blank.

Then it came to me. She knew everything. She had been gardening that afternoon and had heard a commotion in the ravine. At first she had thought it was a raccoon or some birds. But then she had heard voices, had walked to the edge of the yard and looked down through the trees. She had gasped at the sight of Aaron on top of me, then watched, with growing shock, the way I had let him kiss me, how I had held him, obviously willing, with both my arms around him.

"He's not so bad. He's kind of cute." Had she seen his mouth against my sweatshirt? I put down my fork and blundered out of my chair. Dad, Raymond and Kitty looked up. "Excuse me," I said. The napkin fell out of my lap. I reached down and picked it up from the floor, folded it carefully twice, so that the monogram was showing. The food I hadn't eaten was crawling on my plate. I didn't look at Bonnie. My father was looking at me, a stern look that said, Sit back down at the table, young lady.

"Faye," he said and raised one eyebrow. I became aware of a dark current of anger inside me, flowing dangerously close to the surface. After all the things he had done, all the people he had hurt, including Bonnie, my mother—including *me*—there he sat at the head of the table, expecting everyone to obey him.

"Faye," he said again.

"I don't feel well."

"Perhaps you're tired from your long afternoon," Bonnie said. Her voice was sarcastic and pinched, as if she were about to announce to the whole table what she had seen me doing.

I had no choice but to sit back down. I unfolded the napkin and draped it across my legs. There was a tremendous weight in the center of my chest. I sat up straight, as rigidly as when Aaron had touched me. I remembered him making those disgusting little "M" sounds and felt his head once again, like a wrecking ball, smashing against my rib cage, trying to get at my heart.

My father was studying me, as if I'd just walked into the room, as if he were meeting me for the first time. He didn't seem to have detected my anger. Rather, he seemed puzzled by my presence.

If I had been standing, my knees would have buckled. My father leaned forward, his elbows on the table. He hadn't quite finished chewing his last bite of food. He pushed a curl back from his forehead and gazed, with those dark eyes, upon me.

"Dad," I said.

He raised his eyebrows.

"I wish you weren't leaving," I blurted.

Bonnie burst into hysterical laughter. She slapped the table with both hands. We all looked at her and she said, "What do you think, that the rest of us are glad he's going away?"

"I don't think that's what she meant," Dad said.

"She sits there, silent, all the time, with those cold, accusing eyes. I can't bear it."

I couldn't say a word, not even to defend myself. I couldn't believe what she was saying.

"She's a child," my father said.

"I'm not a child," I said.

No one disputed my assertion. My father shrugged. Bonnie stared at him with eyes full of hate then began to smooth down her hair. What had I done to make her so angry? Cold, accusing eyes? It simply wasn't true. I'd never accused her of anything. My actions—I could see each one clearly, as if I were watching a movie of myself—had had no effect on Bonnie, her household, her children. In fact, the only real connection that existed between us was that of my father, and if she thought I had some hold over him, she was mistaken. He barely knew I was alive.

Bonnie heaved a great sigh. Dad, after all the commotion, didn't even seem upset. The children, too, acted as if it were a normal Saturday night and after being excused, took their plates to the kitchen, turned on the television and watched an episode of "Daktari."

Bonnie and my father walked up the staircase, leaving the plates and platters on the table. They banged around, as if opening and shutting drawers. Maybe my father was packing. I had heard the sound before, many years ago—it was practically my first memory—and heard my mother crying desperately, pleading with him not to leave. He had yelled at her, "I'm restless, miserable, going out of my mind." Her idea of helping him pack had been to throw everything out of the medicine cabinet. In the morning I found cans of shaving cream and Right Guard deodorant, even a dark ugly stain on the hard wood floor, where a bottle of cologne had shattered. For weeks the upstairs had smelled like my father, long after he was gone.

I was alone at the table. I pushed my plate to one side, folded my arms in front of me and buried my face like a child at school, asked to take a short nap on her desk top. Crash, bang. The thump of a body hitting the floor. Bonnie was trying to physically prevent my father from packing. He was pushing her away from the chest of drawers. She fell onto the floor. She clung to his leg but he shook her off. She lay, sobbing, in a curled-up ball.

Raymond and Kitty laughed at the television show, at Clarence the Cross-Eyed Lion.

The house became deadly quiet. Had my father knocked Bonnie unconscious? Or had they stopped fighting, their chests heaving, tears pouring down their cheeks? My father held out his hands. It's useless to fight, he whispered. He stared at Bonnie then moved across the room, to embrace her, to apologize.

Which were they doing?

I didn't care, I told myself. I didn't care anymore.

✣ ✣ ✣

I woke up in the middle of the night and turned immediately, instinctively, to look out my window. It was completely dark. I lay curled on my side and wondered what had woken me up—a dream I couldn't remember, a noise that didn't repeat itself.

I got out of bed and crept to the bathroom. The door to Raymond's bedroom was open and I looked in on him. He was asleep at the wrong end of the bed, hugging his bear, his thumb in his mouth. All his marbles were scattered across the floor. They gleamed like eyeballs, catching the light from the street. It was strange that he'd left them on the floor.

Usually when he finished playing, he put them away in their special bags and jars.

I closed his door and turned on the bathroom light. Someone had forgotten to flush the toilet. I sat down on the seat and felt under the hair at the back of my neck. It was damp from sweat. A small brown spider scuttled against the corner of the tub. When I got up, I put down the lid of the toilet without flushing it either.

I turned out the light and went back to bed, intending to put myself to sleep by reading with my flashlight. Just as I pulled up the covers, Kitty whimpered and turned. I sat up but all I could see was her black hair splayed across the pillow. I wondered whether or not I should wake her. I got up and walked to her bed, stood over her and waited. She seemed to have quieted down. I leaned over and blew on the back of her neck, imagining she, too, was sweating. She turned onto her back and though her hair covered her face, I could see that her eyes were open. She stared up at me without blinking or speaking. It made me shiver.

"Kitty," I whispered. "You were having a nightmare."

She scooted back to the edge of her bed and held up the covers to invite me in. I crawled in beside her. The pillow was hot where her head had been resting. She snuggled against me, threw her arm around my waist, her leg across my thigh, and burrowed her face into my shoulder. She made funny little noises which sounded at times like giggling, at other times like the purring of a cat.

"Shhh," I said. "You silly girl."

"You're so pretty," she said. "You have golden hair." She stroked it in a curl behind my ear. She propped herself up on one elbow. "I was dreaming about you," she whispered.

I looked into her eyes, which were black and shiny. I was looking into the face of someone who adored me. How had I failed to notice before now?

"I dreamt Mommy and Daddy died and you had to take care of us," she said. "You had to stay here. You could never leave."

She was stroking my arm with her fingers and looking down into my face. The left side of her mouth was still a little swollen from where the baseball had hit her. She was small for her age, and very smart. She had been praised at school for her reading skills and she had won the spelling bee, over children much older than she was. She was the teacher's pet.

She bent down and placed her swollen mouth very lightly upon my cheek. Her eyes were closed. Her eyelashes were so long they fluttered against my skin.

"You could never leave," she repeated as she lifted her mouth away. "You became our mother."

I took her hand and held it inside mine. "You're the pretty one," I said.

She snuggled back down, her face close to my ear. Soon her breathing became regular. I slipped out from between the covers and tucked her in. I walked to the center of the room and stared out the window. Somewhere in the house a board creaked. Someone else was awake.

I stood in the center of the room for a long time, waiting to hear another footstep. I was aware of my nakedness underneath my nightgown. Sweat had gathered under my arms and between my legs. Suddenly I was afraid I had started my period. I pulled up the long skirt of my nightgown and checked with my finger. It was wet but because of the darkness I wasn't sure if it was red, so I put it to the tip of my tongue. It didn't taste like blood. I continued to hold up the skirt and look down at myself, my white thighs and the slight mound, which I didn't like, of my stomach. Then slowly I lifted the nightgown over my head, dropped it on the floor beside me and stood there naked, feeling the chill of the air against my skin.

I touched myself, my throat and chest, my hips and thighs. I was shaking and my arms and legs felt hollow. When I heard another creak, just down the hall, I knew that someone was coming. They were approaching my door, perhaps to open it and look inside. I waited, trembling violently. I wanted to fly into bed and fling the covers over me. I wanted to squat down into a ball and cover myself. But I stood and waited for the door to open.

Another creak, closer this time. Someone was definitely walking down the hall. I thought I heard the whisper of a breath, someone standing outside the door. The glass knob turned and the door moved an inch. I thought I was going to faint. I heard my name being spoken through the crack but the door didn't open any further. I watched for an eternity. Then I heard my name again. "Faye," came the sound of a hoarse whisper.

I walked to the door and put my fingers on the knob. The cold touch of glass seemed to bring me back to my senses. I knew I was in terrible danger, and that if I opened the door, I would be doomed. My heart was beating so hard that the floor beneath my feet was shaking. I raised my eyes from the doorknob to the black slit of the hall, expecting to see an eye, a flash of skin. Who knows what I expected to see?

But all I saw was darkness. There was no one there. I opened the door wide and stood looking out. Had anyone ever been standing at my door? I looked in all the dark corners of the hall, the closed bedroom, bathroom and closet doors. There was no sign of life and yet, I sensed something. Not exactly a smell. It was almost as if I could sense the displacement of air, how space had been disturbed by someone's presence. It was nothing I could put my finger on. But I waited until it died down, until the molecules fell back into place, filled up the space that had been occupied. A chill swept over my entire body and I knew it had been my father. He had seen my strange shining nakedness, and it had made him flee.

✢ ✢ ✢

We stood in our nightgowns and pajamas at the edge of the front porch and watched my father leave. He had called a taxi, which came ten minutes early and waited in the circular driveway. We each kissed my father in turn. Bonnie went last and held him tightly. Her nightgown was wrinkled from sleep but her hair had been combed and still held a little curl.

"Do you have the pictures?" she cried as Dad got into the taxi.

"No," he said and started back out.

"Faye," she said. I turned and ran to the kitchen, grabbed the photos Dad had taken before the party and ran back to the taxi. I handed the pictures to my father. He looked at them sadly, then told the driver he was ready.

After the taxi had pulled away, we scattered into separate parts of the house. I took a shower and got dressed. The poison ivy had sprouted on my right arm. I dotted the rash with calamine lotion and tried, in an exercise of mind over matter, to make the bumps stop itching. It didn't seem horrible that my father was gone. No one had cried, no one was moping. The only indication that something had changed was that everyone seemed extra quiet.

Around six that evening a car pulled into the driveway. I heard it from my bedroom, where I'd been doing homework for school the next day, and walked across the hall to the upstairs window. Aaron Chandler got out of the car and walked up to the front door. He was carrying my boot. I tapped on the pane of the window where I stood. He heard me and looked up.

I raced down the stairs, my geography workbook still in my hand. Aaron had become bold, now that my father was gone. I thought he should have called and asked, not just come to the house, uninvited.

He smiled when I opened the door. "Here's your boot."

"Thanks."

"Are you going to invite me in?"

"No."

"Fine," he said. "I have something to tell you. Why don't we take a drive?"

"I don't want to hear what you have to say." I held my book to my chest.

"I think you do," he said quietly.

I refused to smile or succumb to his flattery. He sighed and scraped the toe of his sneaker against the welcome mat. He had pulled his hair back into a ponytail. His face wasn't unhandsome, I noticed.

He looked me directly in the eye. "My mother's gone, too," he said.

I took a step back. I thought of slamming the door in his face. His expression, in the few moments it took to let the information sink in, didn't change. He was sad, but something told me that despite his sadness, he was going to make the best of it.

I turned and shouted, "I'll be right back," then stepped out of the house, shut the front door and walked towards his car. When he got into the driver's seat and started the engine, I turned and asked, "Is it true?"

Instead of answering, he leaned over and kissed me, a kiss exactly like those he'd given me in the ravine.

"My father's gone to look for them," he said, turning onto the four-lane road that led to his house. "I don't think he's going to find them."

"No," I said. I felt a strange thrill and wondered how long Dad and Judith Chandler had been planning this.

When we pulled into the driveway of his house, Aaron turned off the engine, got out and opened my door for me. "Come in," he said. "You can call home."

"I don't want to talk to them."

"She'll find out soon enough."

"Not from me."

He nodded. For the first time in my life, I felt certain of what I was doing. I sat at the edge of the couch in his living room. The ceiling was hung with track lights, which had been turned down low. There was a huge abstract painting on the wall, with many large, overlapping blocks of color.

"When is your father coming back?"

He shrugged and handed me a heavy leaded tumbler with an inch of amber liquid sloshing in the bottom. I drank it in three quick swallows then followed Aaron into his bedroom, which was small and glowing, like someone's cozy lair. I lay on his bed and watched him take off his clothes. He didn't seem embarrassed, though his shoulders slumped. "I've never done this before," he said.

"It doesn't matter," I said. He sat on the bed and unbuttoned my shirt. I took off my pants myself. I felt slightly bewildered but he didn't hurt me and it was over very quickly. The room glowed all around me. My mind was blank then I thought about my father and I started to cry. I was shaking with sobs.

Aaron kissed the top of my head. When I was quiet, he climbed on top of me and asked, in his sweetest voice, "Can we do it again?"

For a moment I was frightened that he would keep pressing me, that he would always want more and more. But he waited for me to answer and I knew if I'd said no, he would have obeyed me. He would have taken me home.

"Yes," I said, though I worried about Dr. Chandler coming home and finding me in the bedroom. When Aaron rolled over, I got up and dressed quickly. The poison ivy on my arm itched violently. To keep from scratching, I squeezed my hands together.

Aaron fixed me another whiskey, then drove me back to my father's house. Not my father's anymore, now it was Bonnie's house. Poor Kitty and Raymond. I would invite them to Atlanta. After I left, I would write to them and never forget to send them Christmas presents.

"See you tomorrow," Aaron said. My stomach turned with dread at the thought of going to school. Would Aaron sit next to me at lunch? Would he try to hold my hand?

And when would the kids at school find out about my father? All of a sudden I had a vivid picture of him—by the lake, playing his trumpet, blowing it high in the air. He'd caught sight of Judith Chandler running down the path. There was a glint in his eye like the glint of the moonlight on his trumpet. No wonder he had gone off and left his family. That night he had been happy, wild, expectant; he had summoned her and she had come. I would never forget that image of my father. It was like a snapshot I would always carry with me.

Aaron leaned over and kissed me goodbye, a light kiss on the cheek. When I got out of the car, Bonnie was watching me from an upstairs window. Her face was distorted through the glass—misshapen, her mouth half smiling. We stared at each other then I went into the house, walked straight to the kitchen, called my mother and told her I was coming home.

Ann Scott Knight has worked as a freelance writer and journalist in New York City, Santa Cruz, and Paris. She received degrees from The University of California at Santa Cruz and The MFA Program for Writers at Warren Wilson College. She lives in Manhattan with her husband and son.

The NicolaTatiana King Series

With the publication of Ann Scott Knight's *Hurry Home*, the Nicola Tatiana King Series has been established in memory of the painter and avid reader of short fiction who died in 1995, at age thirty-two. Nicola was born in London and lived with her family in Ireland, Italy, Switzerland and Princeton, New Jersey. She was educated at The International School of Geneva, Dean Junior College, Parsons School of Design in Paris, and received a Bachelor of Fine Arts degree from Parsons/ New York. This series is dedicated to publishing short story collections and novellas by emerging writers of exceptional talent.